POWER CURRENCY

James P Rogers

i

JAMES ROGERS

James Rogers

jim@rogers.cn
rogers@p2pelectric.com

www.powercurrency.net
www.kwcash.com

Covers and Illustrations: Ting He and Cong Yu

ISBN 978-0-9798559-0-0

AXL, Inc. (www.axlinc.com)

POWER CURRENCY

JAMES ROGERS

CONTENTS

TABLES AND FIGURES

INTRODUCTION

The town went through an economic depression. The local manufacturing plant shut down. Money was leaving the community. Unemployment was over 10 percent and the jobs remaining were low paying. Most people in the town with mortgages owed more than the home was worth. Foreclosures were at a record high. The schools and the city budgets were deep in the red.

In this environment, the town adopted alternative currencies. These currencies were backed by land, labor and energy. The town issued loans against future production to help entrepreneurs get a start. The people and town set up local energy systems and used electricity credits as money. People laid off from the factory found new jobs or set up workshops making small energy systems.

People agreed to payment part in Federal Reserve dollars, and part in local currency backed by electricity production. As the local currency was accepted by many merchants for goods, and the county for some taxes, it circulated well. Many businesses earned more electric currency credits than they could use. With this, they went and consumed in the local economy. The grocer accepted the credits, and used them to pay the bills for his store and power for his shop. Soon, he had an excess of electricity credits and used these to pay his own employees as part of their wages and benefits. He used some to pay his own suppliers who in turn used the credits toward their own delivery vehicles. The local car dealer saw an excellent opportunity and established a new business converting old cars to hybrid electric vehicles. He took payment in paper money as well as electric currency. Soon he built his own wind generators, and then bundled electricity credits with the car sales.

Entrepreneurs built biomass plants which process community waste to make fuel. This stored energy feeds into the local electricity grid during peak hours. As time went on, they were able to build a large production base of electricity generation and even augment the pensions with electricity currency. They funded social programs for schools and elderly with the new money. In short, the town became self-sufficient and prospered.

They reclaimed their wealth and freedom.

POWER CURRENCY

Facebook, Groupon, Farmville, Google, Twitter, Paypal - the hot new economy. These great enterprises came from an idea, and spread like wild-fire. There was some venture funding, but for the most part, these internet driven ventures all grew from an entrepreneur's dream and tapped into the 21st Century rulebook. These are all great ideas, and a lot of the growth is driven by using some form of new alternative currency – facebook credits, groupons, game cash, adsense, and so forth. This currency motivates people to enter into that alternative economy and participate. The hyper-growth of these companies reflect that.

Right now, electricity is used as an alternative currency in many US States through 'net metering' laws. We can do more. Using the technology we have now, we can develop a new money - money that is backed by energy.

With this new currency, we can wipe out debt, unemployment, poverty, and oil imports. Power Currency can lead to increasing the economy 100 times in our lifetime, and get us out of the 20th Century Drill for Oil economy and into the 21st Century Outer Space economy.

Right now we have installed capacity of just over one million MWH of electricity potential. China is building 500 thousand MWH capacity in just the next five years[i]. This is half of the capacity that the USA has built all during the 20th Century. The US Energy Information Agency thinks the USA will have an average growth rate of one percent per year through 2030[ii]. This would bring us up to 1.3 million MWH capacity. This is far too small. Using some of the strengths of Facebook, Google and Twitter, we can invent our way out of this economic downturn and increase our energy production ten-fold by 2030. The energy and money establishments are controlled by powerful interest groups, but this does not matter. We can make this happen and 95 percent of what we need, is already in our hands now.

The energy situation in the USA offers the biggest opportunity in the history of the world. Oil prices are passing records highs and energy is strictly controlled. Americans are creative and when faced with a tough situation, they invent and work their way out. Stressful times bring about great innovation.

Money is a human creation. Anything can be money if people put a value on it and it is accepted as a medium of exchange.

It is normal for money to change with the times. Normally, there is a dominant currency (such as Federal Reserve notes in the USA), then there can be all kinds of other types of money. In the USA, we tend to use only one type of money – the dollar, but there have been all kinds of money through history.

	Government	Alternatives
17th Century	Gold, Silver, Copper	Wampum, Beads
	Colonial Paper Money	Corn, wheat
	Continental Dollars	Tea, Sugar
18th Century	Silver Dollars	Hours of skilled labor
	Gold Eagles	Tobacco
	Copper Pennies	Iron, Steel
19th Century	State Bank Notes	Whiskey
	US Notes (Greenbacks)	Casino Chips
	Gold Certificates	Commercial Paper
	Silver Certificates	Company Scrip
20th Century		Bus tokens
	Federal Reserve Notes	Store Coupons
		Stamps
		Military Scrip
		Community Scrip
		Baseball tickets
		Airline miles/tickets
		Phone minutes
		Liberty Dollars
		College credit hours
		Disney Dollars
21st Century		Paypal money
		Facebook Credits
		Virtual game money
		Google credits
		Net Metering (kwh)

1.1 Types of money in America

How many of these types of money in Table 1.1 do you use? No doubt you can add a few more to the list. Not everyone will agree that facebook credits are a form of money. However, the people who use facebook credits to transact a deal certainly see it as money and use it as money. Now, so much of our society is dependent on energy.

The earliest form of money was straight one to one barter. Salt, copper, bronze, shells, gold, silver, rum, tobacco, grains, animals were all used. Farmers would trade their harvest for animal skins for example. Barter was not convenient as you needed to find someone to accept what you had to offer.

As society grew and became more complex, this arrangement was impractical. One of the innovations was the merchant who opened a general store. He stocked all the things the town might need. The farmers, traders, and housewives went there to buy and trade things as needed - cinnamon, sugar, boots, bread, coats, and canes. Still they could carry out barter of goods but they had more options regarding the things they could buy.

From this, the merchant would find there was a certain commodity which had general acceptance in the community. Tobacco was used as money in Virginia during colonial times. In other places, you might see corn used as money. It all evolved from social norms. People found a certain item that served best for their community. Throughout history, gold and silver have fit nicely as a medium of exchange. Gold and silver will always be good as money and there will always be a call to have money that is backed by gold or silver.

We could certainly have electricity and energy backed money, if people will agree to it.

New types of money can come because of innovation. Airline miles are an example of this. Some tech savvy teens and young adults use the new forms of virtual money. Facebook was built on top of the virtual money system, and is monetizing into traditional money later. In any case, it has to be accepted by people using the money, as the medium of exchange.

In times of trouble, people will come up with new forms of money out of necessity. The USA saw thousands of communities use community issued scrip during hard times. During the Banking Panic of 1907, there was a terrible shortage of money in the USA. Instead of general collapse, people found ways to use new forms of money. Clearinghouse currencies in small denomination were marked "payable through the clearinghouse" and the member banks agreed to accept them. Negotiable cashier's checks were written in 5, 10, or 20 dollar amounts and were payable to some person or entity, "John Smith" or "bearer" or such. These were technically illegal but accepted by the population. Companies paid employees in large numbers of small amounts of scrip. The scrip was the liability of the company issuing it, and was passed from hand to hand as a form of money. Some streetcar companies paid their employees in streetcar tokens and tickets. These circulated well as they had value as streetcar rides. In 1907, banks went along with this as it helped to prevent runs on banks. People used alternative currencies and did not need to withdraw so much money from the bank. With a severe shortage of money in the city, people figured out how to deal with the situation.

Alternative currencies will always be accepted and work quite well if the people agree to use them. Most of these alternative currencies in 1907 were technically illegal. Everyone knew they were illegal, but nobody did anything about it. Part of the reason was the lack of currency, but also, the use was so widespread that the government could not stop it. To government bureaucrats and collectivists, this was a nightmare. This competes with establish centrally controlled money. [iii]

We can further classify money into fiat and commodity. People accept fiat paper money because they are forced to by the King or Government, and they feel confident they can use it later to purchase what they need. If people lose faith in the money or there is too much paper money, then that money becomes worthless. We see this during times of trouble such as with the US Confederate States, Weimar Germany, China in the 1940's, and now in Zimbabwe. Our Federal Reserve dollars we use now are fiat paper money.

Commodity money is often called 'hard money'. If there was a disaster, and the Federal Reserve dollars we use now have no value, what would you use for money? When economies break down, people tend to move to money that is commodity backed such as gold, silver, tobacco, tea, corn, jade, rice, etc... Commodity money itself has intrinsic value. In some situations, an apple or gallon of water would be worth more than a pound of gold.

It is worthwhile to go back to Table 1.1 and write in a few notes. If your State is under financial duress, think of new types of money they can use. As long as people will accept it, then it can be used as a sort of money. If there is a collapse in the paper money, what will you use for money?

If you listen to the media, you hear that loss of the paper money would lead to loss of money itself. This is propaganda. The money will change to something else. If you are a doctor, dentist, carpenter, or plumber you will be fine. If you are a lawyer or college professor, you may or may not do so well. If you are a farmer, and can control your land, then your land and crops will be fine as money. Sorry to say but people with guns will do better than people without guns.

There is also paper money that is backed by some commodity, which falls in between. Examples in Table 1.1 are U.S. Dollar Gold and Silver Certificates.

Previously in Table 1.1 we listed types of money. Below are the levels of money supply during the 19th to 20th Century. Today we only think of one kind of money – the Federal Reserve Dollar. This is not normal. Prior to 1970, there were a lot of different types of money. There was hard commodity money, United States Dollars and Federal Reserve Dollars.

This data in Table 1.2 comes from the US Statistical Abstracts which you can find on the Census site[iv].

	Hard Money		United States Money		Bank Money	
	Gold & Silver	Coins	Gold & Silver Certificates	Green-backs	Bank Notes	Federal Reserve Dollars
	No debt		No debt		**Debt**	
1800	16				10	
1810	27				28	
1820	22				45	
1830	26				61	
1840	79				107	
1850	147				131	
1860	228				207	
1870	90		32	325	328	
1880	294		13	328	337	
1890	485		429	335	182	
1900	753	26	609	318	375	0
1910	800	46	1282	335	687	0
1920	801	91	357	278	691	3,065
1930	677	117	1382	288	652	1,402
1940	430	159	1649	248	166	5,163
1950	1125	370	2218	321	88	22,760
1960	1760	549	2157	318	57	27,094
1970	5002	1,126	225	297	29	47,627
1980	0	1,500	0	100	0	117,400
1990	0	2,000	0	0	0	254,400
2000	0	2,500	0	0	0	549,300
2010	0	3,000	0	0	0	873,300

1.2 19th and 20th Century Money, in millions Source: Figures for coins, silver and greenbacks are estimated 1980 – 2010. Source: US Statistical Abstract and Federal Reserve Bank

You can see that the money supply was somewhat steady until about 1970. In fact, it was very difficult to inflate. The money was fixed to silver and gold. We needed to dig it out of the ground so there was a natural limit on currency inflation. If there was too much silver in the economy, it would find its way overseas in exchange for silk, tea, spices, and other goods. There is no such limit to paper money, especially in the computer age.

You can also see a clear shift in our money from debt free over to 99 percent debt. The Federal Reserve Dollars come from money that is loaned into the economy. Note the enormous growth in the amount of Federal Reserve Dollars in the past few decades. These new types of Federal Reserve Dollars can simply be printed, and if they run out of paper, they can put the values in the computer or put bigger numbers on the paper bills.

Through our history there was a shift in types of money

1620 to 1913. Money is primarily commodity backed. Most of the money that came into circulation was produced in the form of gold and silver. There were other forms of money in colonial times. Most money is debt free, while debt money is used for mortgages and commerce.

1913 to 1965. There is a steady shift from United States dollars to Federal Reserve dollars: debt-free money to debt based money.

1965 to 2008. Debt free US dollars are eliminated and close to 100 percent of money is Federal Reserve Dollars backed by US Government debt.

2008 to today. Money today is backed by US Government debt, subprime mortgages and bad commercial debt.

There is a huge inflation in money supply. In the 1950's there was still some restraint on the printing of money but by 2008 this restraint has died. Now, most of this money is not printed; it is put into the bank's computers as digits. It is too easy for the Federal Reserve to make money now, and this causes fast growth in money inflation and price inflation.

Besides water, can you think of a commodity used by more people than energy? Everyone uses electricity. The Census says there are 111 million homes in America, and 111 million homes use electricity. If we can find a way to use energy – especially electricity - as a medium of exchange, then we have a money for the 21st Century. It has the commodity advantages that gold and silver have, and has the widespread use that paper money has. In Table 1.2 if we extend to the future, Power Currency would fall into the category of 'Hard Money'.

Of course the biggest drawback is we cannot really store watt hours, or kilowatt hours. To fix this, we consider Power Currency to have three components.

Machines – steam turbines, nuclear power, PV cells, wind turbine, generator, car engine, ship engines and farm machines.

Fuels – oil, coal, biomass, sunlight (if harnessed), bio-diesel, ethanol, gas, wood, and waste.

Electricity – the making, delivery and use of electricity.

Electricity us used by everyone but cannot be stored. Fuel can be stored, and could be used to back money but is difficult to distribute except through centralized means. Engines cannot really be used as money but they are a good alternative to gold and silver as an asset. Working together, engines, fuel and electricity can provide the foundation for a new type of money. We will go into detail how this works later in the book.

Economic textbooks say that money has three characteristics – medium of exchange, unit of account, and standard of value. In this chapter we covered medium of exchange - money has to be accepted and valued by society. We will cover unit of account and standard of value later in the next chapter. Electricity is used by everyone but can we figure a way to make it the basis for money.

You say, 'Stop! 'We can't do that! You are messing with THE MAN, the IRS, Uncle Sam, Big Oil, Wall Street! They will never allow it! I want my money back!'

You are right, we need to make sure things are legal. You see the 'Liberty Dollar' in Table 1.1. The founder of that is in jail. He went a bit too far and challenged both the money monopoly and the Government. These proposals assume that the necessary legal steps are done. Congress can pass laws. States can issue money under some restrictions. Some alternative monies can exist if done the proper way.

Now, with modern technology and our energy backed economy, kilowatt hours can be a new widely accepted form of money. As an alternative money, it could be as legal as facebook credits or Disney dollars – it is tolerated. As a Government backed money, it can have the strength of gold and the acceptance of paper money. Many States already allow some very limited form of this through 'Net Metering' or 'feed in tariffs' where electric utilities are required to purchase excess energy from homeowners who have solar energy systems. It would not take too much to take this to the next level. It has the potential to change the game and the economy.

I make the case for Power Currency as a national currency that replaces our existing money system.

DOLLARS and FROLLARS

Money needs to be a 'Unit of Account' that is recognized by all parties. It needs to be divisible without destroying value, and have the same value in different places. It needs to have a specific weight, measure and size. A one ounce gold coin will be accepted in London or Beijing as being a one ounce gold coin.

In the 18th Century, the U.S. States had their own coins, paper money, banks and policies. There were many different currencies in circulation – pesatas, francs, pounds, and sovereigns. There was scrip issued by states, cities, or large companies. It was a money changer's dream. This was chaos but it worked to a large degree.

At the time, the Spanish dollar was 377 grains of silver. It was the most used coin in the colonies. In 1792, Congress wrote and President George Washington signed the Coinage Act which determined the exact composition of the dollar. Silver was the primary unit of measure and gold was derived from its relation to silver. Alexander Hamilton measured a basket of dollars and took the average. As the dollars were worn out a bit, the content was a bit less so the US dollar was set at 371.25 grains of silver.

	Dollars	Gold	Silver
		grains	grains
Eagles	10.00	247.500	
½ Eagles	5.00	123.750	
¼ Eagles	2.50	61.875	
Dollars	1.00		371.250
½ Dollars	0.50		185.625
¼ Dollars	0.25		92.812
Dimes	0.10		37.125
Nickels	0.05		18.587

2.1 Gold and silver specifications

Note: 1 ounce = 437.5 grains and one pound = 7000 grains

Gold coins were called EAGLES, and the EAGLES had a relative value to the dollar. In that same Act, President Washington signed into law a death penalty for anyone who counterfeited money or debased the coins. Here from the Coinage Act of 1792:

> Section 19. And be it further enacted, That if any of the gold or silver coins which shall be struck or coined at the said mint shall be debased or made worse as to the proportion of the fine gold or fine silver therein contained, or shall be of less weight or value than the same out to be pursuant to the directions of this act, through the default or with the connivance of any of the officers or persons who shall be employed at the said mint, for the purpose of profit or gain, or otherwise with a fraudulent intent, and if any of the said officers or persons shall embezzle any of the metals which shall at any time be committed to their charge for the purpose of being coined, or any of the coins which shall be struck or coined at the said mint, **every such officer or person who shall commit any or either of the said offenses, shall be deemed guilty of felony, and shall suffer death.**[v]

So there we have it, the Government put a penalty of death on anyone who worked to debase the currency.

In 1792, the proportional value of gold and silver was set at 15 units of pure silver to 1 unit of pure gold. Standard gold was defined as 11 parts pure gold to one part alloy composed of silver and copper. As long as both were used for money there was a natural ratio of silver and gold. Over time, there were some adjustments made to the coinage to account for changes in the balance of international trade. Still, Congress was able to control itself because it worked within the constraints of gold and silver. There was some inflation and deflation in the money, but overall, the money stayed pretty consistent in value over a long period of time.

	Dollar (grains silver)	Eagle (grains gold)	Silver: Gold
April 2, 1792	371.25	247.5	15 to 1
June, 1834	371.25	232	16 to 1
January 18, 1837	206.25	258	8 to 1
February 12, 1873	378	258	14.6 to 1

2.2 Gold:Silver Ratios

Even until 1857 foreign gold and silver coins were allowed as legal money. Anyone could bring in silver, and government put it into a form that all of the economy could agree upon.

The silver came from the people. People could take the silver to a mint where it was coined into very exact sizes, weights and mixed with exact amounts of alloys. Anyone could go out and dig up gold and silver, or conduct trade to attain silver, then bring it to a mint to be coined. The laws were focused on the weights and measures of the money. The government was there to provide a service to mint coins and ensure there was a 'unit of account'. They opened up the minting of silver to all people, and to allow foreign coins to be used. The first mint was established in Philadelphia in 1792 and we now have mints in San Francisco (1854), Denver (1906), and West Point (1973). It was too troublesome to ship the gold to Philadelphia to mint so the Government also had mints established in Charlotte, North Carolina (1838–1861) and Dahlonega, Georgia (1838–1861) to mint local gold deposits into gold coins. Andrew Jackson set up a mint in New Orleans, (1838– 1909) to help people in the South and West. It minted gold and silver in all denominations. Carson City (1870 - 1893) was set up primarily for silver coins. There have been private mints especially during gold rushes. These private mints would coin gold or silver to US specifications and the money was circulated just as if the Government did minted the coins.

This unit of account lasted until the Coinage Act of 1965. This cut the US dollar 'unit of account' with silver. In the 1960's gold started to break its 'unit of account' with the dollar until August 1971 when the dollar cut all ties with any gold or silver. Go back to Table 1.2 and you see that prior to 1970, the amount of US dollars was steady, and since 1970 there is a terribly fast rise in the amount of Frollars in circulation.

The final characteristic of money is 'standard of value'. Money must be able to be compare values over time. So money paid today will be valued at some similar measurable form at some time in the future. It can be readily stored and retrieved so that people can save it long term. As such, it needs to be stable and not be inflated away into nothing[vi]. This is the biggest challenge with Power Currency as electricity cannot be stored. We address this in a bit.

Taking the total money supply from Table 1.2, divide that by the total population in the United States, then take a look at the money per person and price index (inflation).

	Money Supply (millions)	Money Supply per Person	Price Index (1913=100)
1860	435	14	71
1870	775	20	102
1880	972	19	83
1890	1,431	23	78
1900	2,081	27	80
1910	3,150	34	97
1920	5,283	50	200
1930	4,518	37	167
1940	7,815	59	140
1950	26,882	178	241
1960	31,935	178	296
1970	54,306	267	388
1980	119,600	528	824
1990	257,500	1,035	1,307
2000	553,300	1,959	1,722
2010	879,300	2,855	2,177

2.6 Money Supply and Inflation

Source for Price Index: Statistical Abstracts, Bureau of Economic Analysis

We get a strong relationship between the growth of money and rise in prices. Who has not seen the prices of gasoline, food, housing, and such items increase over time? Chocolate bars were a nickel and now a dollar. With a dollar you could buy a coffee and the Sunday newspaper. Greenspan, Bernanke, Geitner and mainstream economists will say that inflation comes from short term trends and daily events like a droughts civil unrest, China's booming economy. Those events might affect prices for a day, week or year, but over a long period of time, currency inflation causes price inflation. If they print trillions of extra dollars to bailout banks, then we will see an amount of inflation about equal to that increase in money supply. They get the extra money, you pay the higher prices.

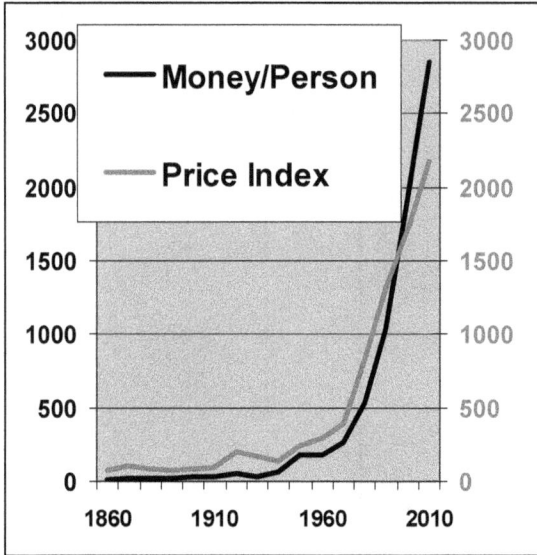

2.7 Graph, money and prices

Look at the curve in Graph 2.7 and imagine the future. At some time in the future – it is inevitable - we will see a pound of coffee costing 1,000 dollars, homes selling for billions, rent for a one bedroom apartment costing one million dollars – in Camden New Jersey.

All it takes to destroy the money is a consistent inflation rate over a long period of time. The Consumer Price Index fits an exponential curve. The rate at which the CPI is growing year-by-year is calculated mathematically by the equation:

$$y_1 = y_0(1+r)^n$$

y0 is the CPI at the start of a certain period of time

y1 is the CPI at the end of the period of time

r is the annual growth rate of the CPI during the period of time

N is the time period in years.

Here is how it looks if we fit it to an exponential curve starting in 1913.

16

The smooth curve is growing three percent per year and the dotted curve is the actual price inflation according to the Bureau of Labor Statistics. You can see that inflation was moderate and has taken off like a rocket in just the past few decades.

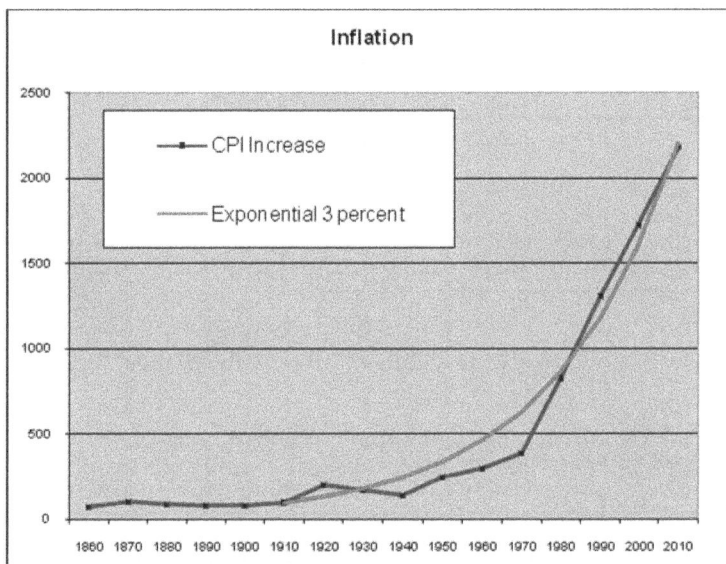

2.8 Inflation is exponential

This translates into gold prices. This is the benefit to owning precious metals. You hear a lot about the need to buy gold and silver. It is not that the gold or silver is getting more valuable. The issue is that there is a flood of new paper money on the market but the amount of gold and silver on the market is about the same. The value of each paper dollar is getting less and less. If you buy and hold gold or silver, in a few decades you will have maintained some level of wealth.

Let's look at the price of gold in relation to silver and oil. In general, it takes about 40 ounces of silver to equal one ounce of gold, and it takes about 15 barrels of oil to equal one ounce of gold. We can predict this ratio out into the future. The ratios to silver and oil will fluctuate some but remain in some consistent band.

17

	Gold	Silver	Oil
1950	1	47	20
1960	1	38	18
1970	1	20	20
1980	1	29	17
1990	1	80	16
2000	1	56	9
2010	1	40	12
2020	1	30 to 60	10 to 20
2030	1	30 to 60	10 to 20
2040	1	30 to 60	10 to 20
2050	1	30 to 60	10 to 20

2.9 Gold: Silver: Oil

This chart shows the dollar prices of gold and oil over the past century.

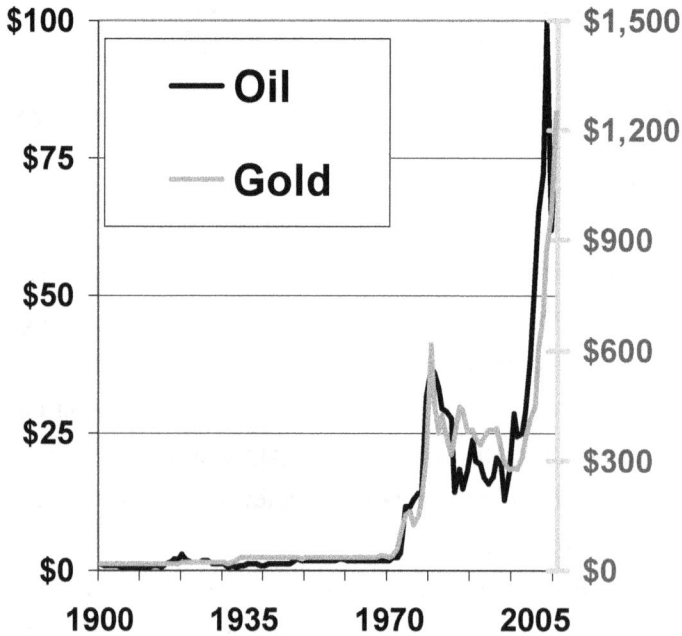

2.10 Oil and Gold   Source for data: US Geological Survey, Energy Information Administration

There is a simple theory about why there is a fairly constant ratio among these commodities. These things take effort to bring out of the ground. They are not so easy to find and are finite. All these factors give a restriction to commodities that you don't see with paper money. In the future we could see a cup of coffee cost $10,000 dollars, but we will not see a cup of coffee cost one ounce of gold. There is no limit to paper money. Paper money can be printed and have numbers put on the paper.

But, what about making gold and silver money again? Gold and Silver are excellent forms of money, and they will always be money. Many States are looking at gold and silver backed money. The problem in the 21st Century economy is that gold and silver are used in many electronics products and we have a problem with hoarding. Let's look at this.

In 1792, there was not as much opportunity to hoard as developed later with faster sea travel. In the period of a few days, a whole year's production of gold can be moved anywhere around the globe and put into vaults. Billions of dollars are spent each year to extract the 2500 to 3000 tons that is mined each year. If you put all the gold ever mined (160,000 tons) into a football stadium and covered the area within the goalposts and sidelines, the height would be less than three feet. If you then add the yearly total to this, the amount of gold would be a sheet slightly thicker than half an inch.

The USA has 8,192 tons of gold stored in vaults at Fort Knox, West Point, and the Federal Reserve Bank of New York. This averages out to about one ounce per person in the USA and it all can fit into a cube about the size of one 900 square foot apartment with a ten foot ceiling. It could be put on one ship and carried off in one day. That is the main weakness of a gold standard. If we go back to the gold standard for our money, it will be too easy to manipulate and would provoke war in some extreme cases.

In China there are gold shops popping up all over. The people buy the gold, but they will not spend the gold. It is being hoarded. It is used in gifts and jewelry, but never to transact normal everyday things.

Electricity as 'Hard' Money

Now, lets look at electricity. Here is the price of electricity in terms of dollars.

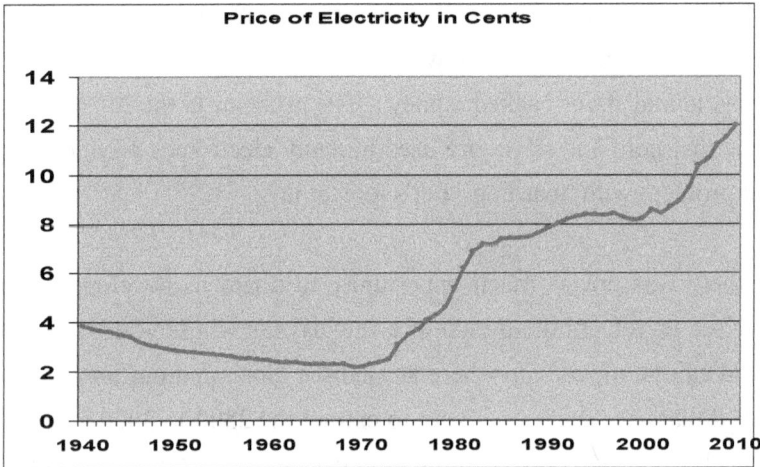

2.11 Electricity in cents

You see the trend by now - the big inflation started around the early 1970s and has gone up about four percent each year. Well, that does not look so good. How can we use electricity as a standard of value if the value keeps changing? There is no way to predict the future, and the value of our money would drop quickly over time.

It is the depreciation of the dollar that is the issue here. In terms of gold, the price of electricity is quite steady. In fact, electricity in terms of gold or silver gets a little bit cheaper each year, reflecting the technology. Things like computers, mobile phones and such get cheaper – the same is true of electricity priced in relation to gold and silver.

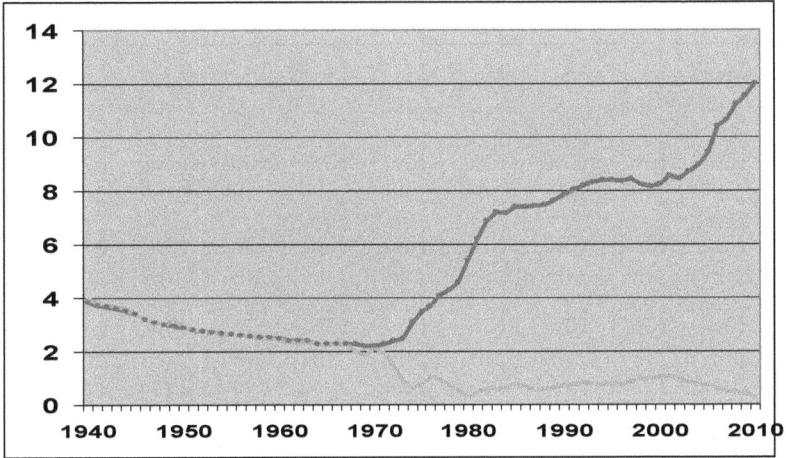

2.12 Electricity and Gold

Here is a look at the prices of common items - electricity, gasoline, Flour, beef, bacon and apples. We put all items in a chart and compare them to the dollar with 1980 as our base year. The prices of all items rose **in terms of Federal Reserve Dollars**.

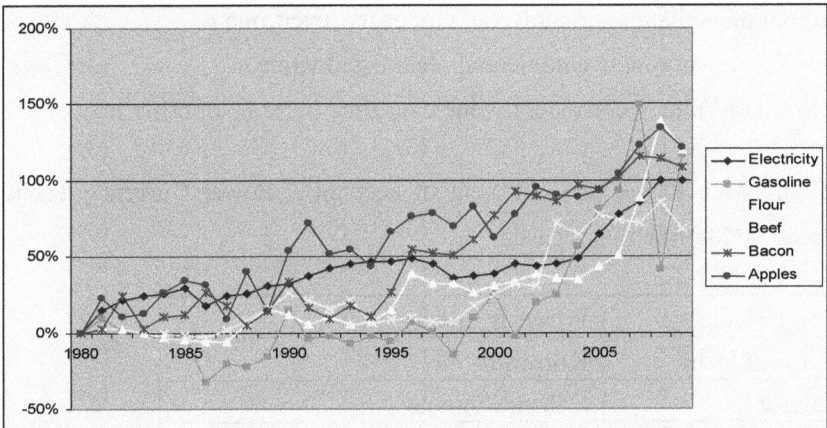

2.13 Food and Energy items vs. dollar

Here are the same items but now priced in terms of electricity. We simply do a series of ratios to get this. The price fluctuation over a period of thirty years is quite stable. Electricity as a standard of value over time is stronger than the paper money we use now.

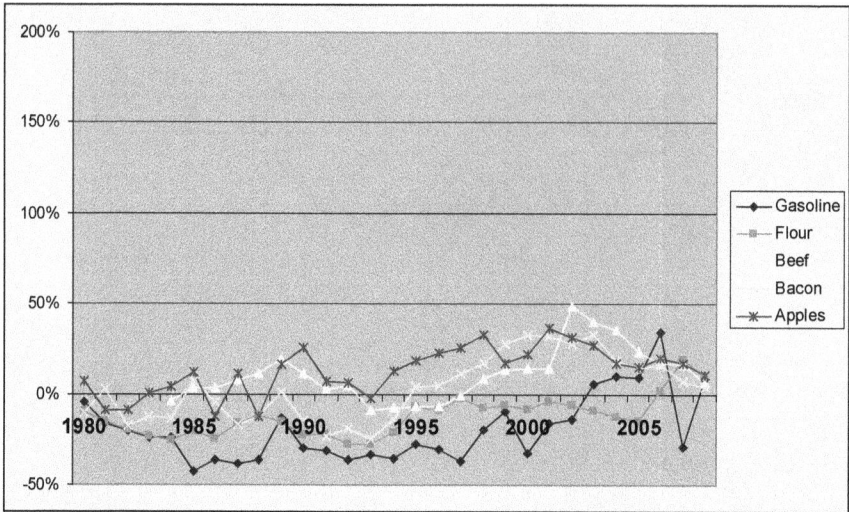

2.14 Electricity vs. food and energy items

There is some variation, but the numbers tend to stay constant. Electricity maintains a nice steady stability in prices. Electricity meets the theoretical requirements of money:

Medium of exchange – widely used by nearly everyone

Unit of Account – indisputable and recognized value

Standard of Value – consistent value over time in terms of other items

Let's go back to the issue of 'unit of account'. Power Currency has its greatest strength in this regard.

Energy Units	Power is Energy Flow
Kilowatt Hour	Kilowatts
Calorie	Calories/minute
BTU	BTU/second or BTU/hour
joule	joule/sec = watt
Horsepower hour	Horsepower/hour

2.3 Energy Units

Just like ounces of gold or silver, energy and power measurements are recognized the same by everyone around the world.

1 joule = 0.239 calories (cal)

1 calorie = 4.187 joules (J)

1 British thermal unit (Btu) = 1055 joules

1 Quad = 1000 trillion Btu, approximately 172 million barrels of oil equivalent (boe)

Each of these measures is convertible to the other.

BTU	British Thermal Unit -- can raise the temperature of one pound of water one degree Fahrenheit
Cal	Large or kilogram calorie -- can raise the temperature of one kilogram of water one degree Celsius
cal	Small or gram calorie -- One cal can raise one gram of water one degree Celsius
ft-lb	The energy exerted by a force of one pound moving one foot
KW-hr	Energy to run a 1000 watt appliance for one hour
joule	The energy exerted by a force of one newton moving one meter

1 watt = 1.0 joule/second = 3.413 Btu/hr

1 kilowatt (kW) = 3413 Btu/hr = 1.341 horsepower

1 MW (mW) = 1,341 horsepower

1 kilowatt-hour (KWH) = 3.6 MJ = 3413 Btu

1 horsepower (hp) = 550 foot-pounds per second = 2545 Btu per hour = 745.7 watts = 0.746 kW

2.4 Conversions

To further illustrate the conversions between the various measures, lets convert to food. The energy in food is measured in calories, which is convertible to BTU's and Kilowatt hours.

		Calories	BTU	KWH
McDonalds cheese-burger		320	1270	0.372
McDonalds french fries		645	2560	0.750
Beer	350ml	151	599	0.176
Apples	100g	59	234	0.069
Banana	100g	92	365	0.107
Hershey's chocolate	100g	550	2183	0.640
Bread with grain	slice(32g)	80	318	0.093
Ice cream	100g	126	500	0.147

2.5 Energy: Food

To get one KWH of energy you could eat:

> a hamburger and large fries
>
> or a six pack of beer
>
> or one and half chocolate bars
>
> or fifteen apples.

If you are ten pound overweight, that is about 35000 calories, or about forty kilowatt hours or about 20 gallons of beer.

Congress can establish money that has energy as its backing. This falls in line with the strict weights and measures that we saw back in 1792. People can use it as a barter tool to regulate value. States could set up currency systems with energy backing, though they may need to mix in come gold and silver to satisfy the demands of the Constitution.

ENGINES, FUELS, ELECTRICITY

The United States is the wealthiest country in the world. A huge part of the wealth is due to energy production and consumption and gold old 20th Century fossil fuels have been the key reason. Oil, gas and coal are the big three that have powered the nation. Prior to the 19th Century most energy came from the sun, flowing streams, and biomass – wood and waste. Prior to the 20th Century most work was done with muscle power. We see terms like horsepower, etc... With the industrial revolution and the steam engine, our living standards have risen. The advances we have made through history correlates with the amount of energy which we harness and use.

Electric power transformed our lives. To a large extent, electricity defines modern technological civilization. The reasons may not be easy to appreciate for those who have never known the filth, toil, and danger associated with obtaining and using such fuels as wood, coal, and whale oil.

Energy Consumption by Source

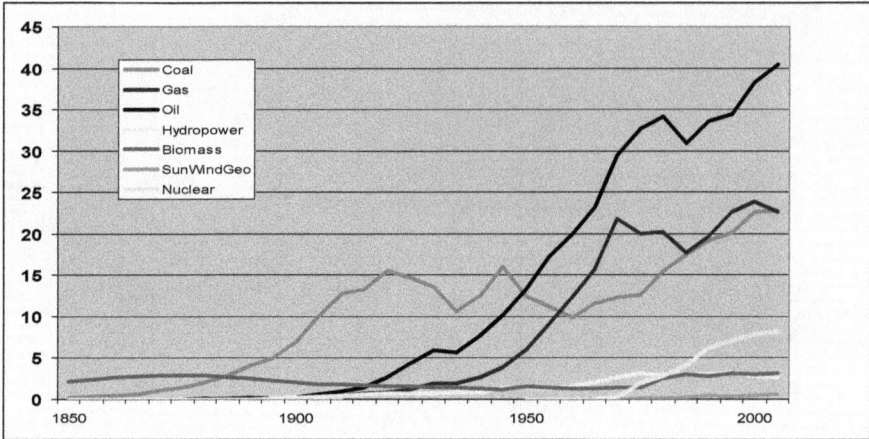

3.1 Energy history

Source: DOE

Annual Energy Review 2008.

Now, electricity is clean, flexible, controllable, safe, effortless, and instantly available. In homes, it runs everything from toothbrushes and televisions to heating and cooling systems. Outdoors, electricity guides traffic, aircraft, and ships, and lights up the night. Electricity is an essential part of our life. Just look at the problems we suffer during ice storms and blackouts. Lack of heating and air conditioning can cause death during extreme weather.

This link with prosperity is well recognized in Asia. China will add 500 gigawatts of electricity capacity between 2011 and 2016 and it will put China far ahead of any country in the world. The USA was on such a growth curve, but recent growth has slowed to a trickle. Instead of doubling every ten years, it was doubling every 35 years and now not even growing. The USA took all the way to 2005 to reach 1000 gigawatts, and we add about 30 or 40 gigawatts each year.

We see a strong relationship between growth in GDP and supply of electricity.

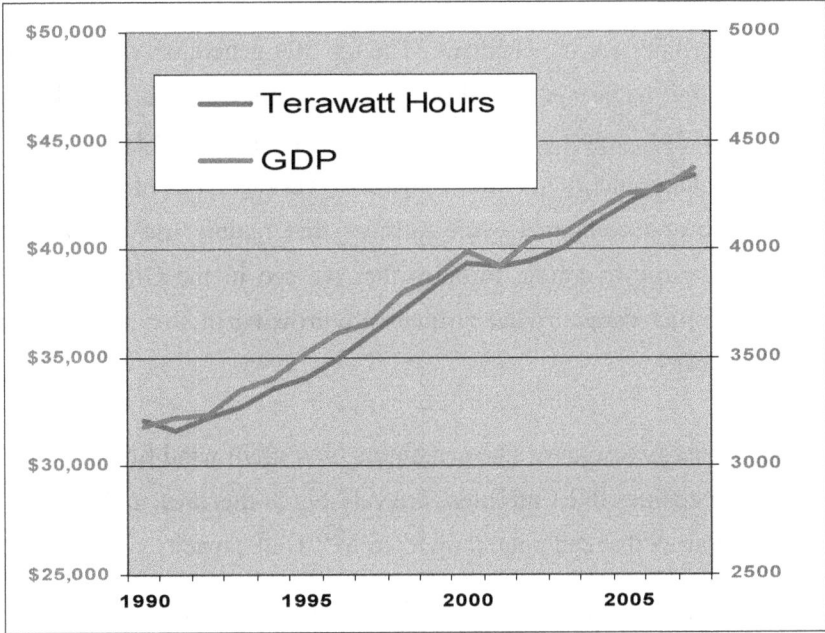

3.2 Energy and GDP

ENGINES

There is about 1,100 Gigawatt Capacity in the USA electric power system. Here is a breakdown by type for the whole national grid in MWH capacity and horsepower.

Type	MWH	Horsepower
Steam Turbines	580,420	778,342,550
Gas Turbines	388,609	521,124,669
Hydro	77,910	104,477,176
Wind	34,683	46,510,171
Pumped Storage	20,538	27,541,860
Other Turbines	18,578	24,913,634
Other Renewable	948	1,270,598
Total	1,121,686	1,504,180,658

3.3 Electricity Prime Movers

The Steam turbines are the elephant. The top 300 generators are all steam turbines running nuclear and coal power plants, but can also run oil, gas, and biomass. The largest turbine is a 1425 MWH (1.425 GWH) steam turbine run by Duke Energy in Ohio. There are various types of combustion (Gas) turbine and combined cycle turbines that mainly use natural gas. Next are the large hydraulic turbines that we see in the Grand Coulee, Hoover and other dams. Wind turbines are growing in size and installations every year.

Distributed energy resources like generators, and small wind fill an important gap. Companies like Caterpillar are very big in this area, and make mobile generators that can put out up to 16 MWH of capacity.

These plants can be developed and put into large buildings, factories, parks, stadiums, etc... Smaller ones are good for homes and stores.

Technology	Size KWH	Installed Cost($/KW)
Diesel Engine	1-10,000	350-800
Natural Gas Engine	1-5,000	450-1,100
Micro turbine	15-60	950-1,700
Combustion Turbine	300-10,000	550-1,700
Fuel Cell	100-250	5,500+
Photovoltaics	0.01-8	8,000-13,000
Wind Turbine	0.2-5,000	1,000-3,000

3.4 Electricity Prime Movers - Small

Dispersed distributed power puts control and decisions into the hands of a greater number of users.

A small percentage of people in any neighborhood are all that is needed to cover emergencies. In times of huge storms, most people can hook up as needed and as fuel allows. It is merely a software issue to assign a unique identifier to each battery, power generator, and other assets so that load balancing can take place. With the heat pumps in homes, solar thermal heaters and other devices, homes become self sufficient. They not only get off the grid but they send energy onto the grid. This concept gets exciting in the future.

FUEL

US oil imports are the largest component of the trade deficit. Until about 1965, we were energy independent, but now we import 60 percent of our oil. Every time someone fills up their gas tank, much of that money leaves the community and goes overseas. Since the attacks on September 11, 2001, we have sent more money to OPEC for crude oil than in all the time from 1900 to 2001.

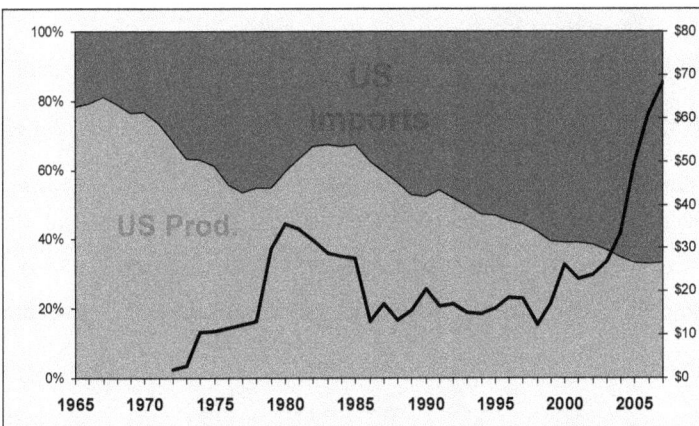

3.5 Fuel imports and prices

You can see in Figure 3.5 that the price of oil also tends to rise, the more that we import. Every time there is trouble in faraway lands, oil supplies are disrupted, and our fuel prices see a jump. A pipeline in Nigeria blows up, our gas price goes up. Trouble with Iran? Prices go up. Instability in Iraq? Prices up. Russia decides to cut off some gas to Europe? Prices up. Locally, we have an oil spill in the Gulf of Mexico? Prices up. All these events give the speculators more opportunities to change the prices up and down. The long term trend for oil prices is up, mainly due to money printing. This is a lot of wealth leaving the country.

You can see in Table 3.1 that the amount of oil we import has grown dramatically since 1970.

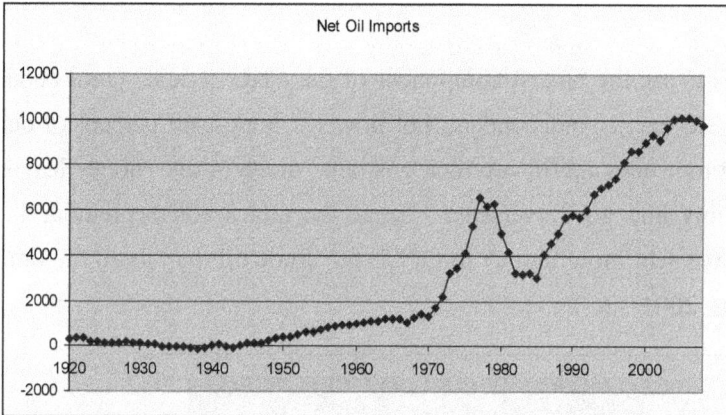

3.6 U.S. Net Imports of Crude Oil (Thousand Barrels per Day)

This trend will get worse if we stay addicted to oil. OPEC has by far the highest level of oil reserves in the world. This gives them control over our prosperity and points to a future where money continues to leave our communities.

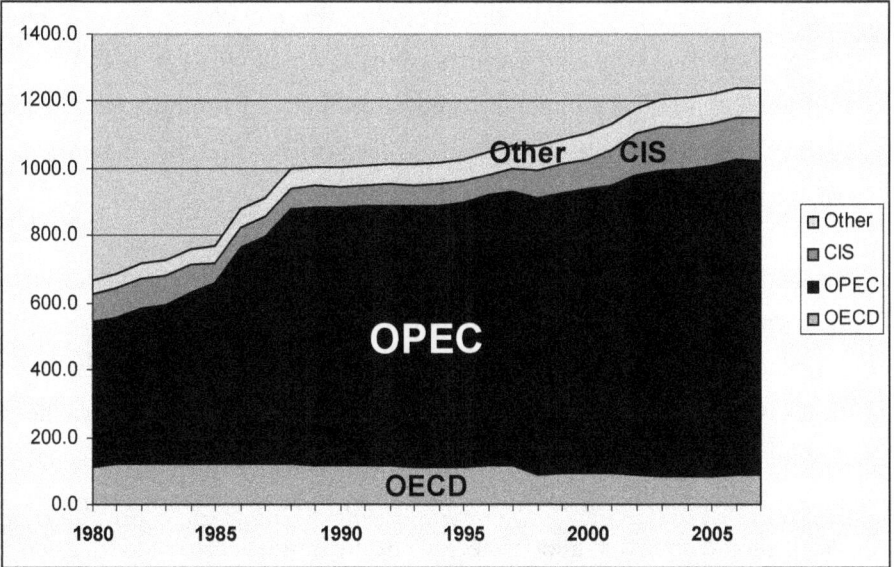

3.7 Oil Reserves, OPEC, CIS – Countries that comprised former Soviet Union Source: British Petroleum Annual Survey

China, India and other countries are putting millions of cars on the road. China's daily consumption of oil has doubled over the past ten years and accounts for half of all the increase in worldwide consumption.

	1999	2009	Change
USA	19,519	18,686	-833
China	4,477	8,625	4,148
India	2,134	3,183	1,049
World	75,648	84,077	8,429

We don't need to convert our vehicles to electric to get away from imported oil. In 1906, farmers worked to cash in on the huge market for fuel by making denatured alcohol for automobile fuel. By using farm wastes they saved money on disposal and had a new cash crop. They formed co-operatives for this purpose with the goal to have community distilleries.

In 1906 Congress passed laws that supported this movement, but had some trickery hidden in the laws. Farmers were required to have inspectors year round and to produce a minimum amount each day. Farming is seasonal so these requirements were nearly impossible to fulfill. Prohibition killed what was left of the movement.

Bio-fuels are ideal as fuels to support Power Currency. They come from the energy of the sun, so they are renewed always. They have the potential to replace crude oil and help with the trade deficit. Bio-diesel can replace diesel 100 percent while ethanol can replace up to 85 percent of gasoline. Biofuels give better engine performance and less pollution. Oil and coal have sulfur, while biofuels have none. They have less CO_2 emissions which should appeal to a lot of people. Some biofuels are made from garbage, sewage, and other wastes. Along with this, biofuel plants can be small in size so that farms, towns and cities can set up their own production. This keeps the money in the community and adds to local wealth.

Diesel gallon	41.420 KWH
Gasoline gallon	36.718 KWH
LNG gallon	27.316 KWH
Propane gallon	26.687+/-1.703 KWH
Ethanol gallon	23.091 KWH
Methanol gallon	17.413 KWH

3.8 Liquid Fuel: KWH Conversions

Many cars and trucks in China, Brazil and other places are able to use a wide variety of fuels – methanol, diesel, bio-diesel, etc... This is out of necessity. The USA has strict controls over which fuels can be used in cars. This is an area where farmers, entrepreneurs, and small energy producers, etc will be able to get very rich.

Storage. Over 99 percent of all electricity is produced, delivered and used immediately. Storage of electricity is very expensive. There are tens of billions in research into energy storage. It is the multi-trillion dollar industry of the next quarter century. Imagine as electricity is produced, the excess is sent to these storage sites. Then as the demand spikes up, or reaches a peak, the consumers can pull from these.

Gasoline	12 KWH/kg
Wood	3.154+/-1.554 KWH/kg
Secondary Lithium-Ion	0.11 KWH/kg
Lead Acid Battery	0.025 KWH/kg
Nickel Metal Hydride	0.06 KWH/kg
Flywheel	0.12 KWH/kg
Storage capacitors	0.5 to 10 W·h/kg
Ice to water	0.0093 KWH/kg

3.9 Energy Storage: KWH Conversions

Some advanced solutions will come from flywheels, nanotechnology, superconducting materials, and hydrogen. Research and Development on batteries is certain to bring some breakthroughs. The key is to increase the density of energy and make them less toxic.

ELECTRICITY

Electricity reaches into nearly every home and business in the country. This huge grid was developed in the 1930's and still serves us today. The high voltage lines are as high as 765,000 volts and then stepped down to 120 volts by the time it reaches the homes. Massive arteries, trunk lines carry very high voltage electricity over hundreds or thousands of miles to the substations which then step it down. The voltage is then transformed downward to between 12,000 and 35,000 Volts. Just before it enters your house, it is again transformed further down to 120-240 volts.

The power companies spend billions each year to manage the load patterns. The delivery of electricity is near instantaneous. Power plants use software to predict the demand patterns for their customers. You can imagine in your own life that you use electricity at a certain pattern. At home you probably use it early in the morning, and then at night. During the weekends it would be throughout the day. Certain major events like major TV shows or sporting events will see a spike in use. Commercial use ramps during the midday. The utilities pull all these patterns together to predict a profile across all customers.

1900 – 2MW plant
1903 – 5MW plant
1905 – 18MW plant
1912 – 35MW plants
1953 - 125 MW plants
1967 – 1000 MW plants

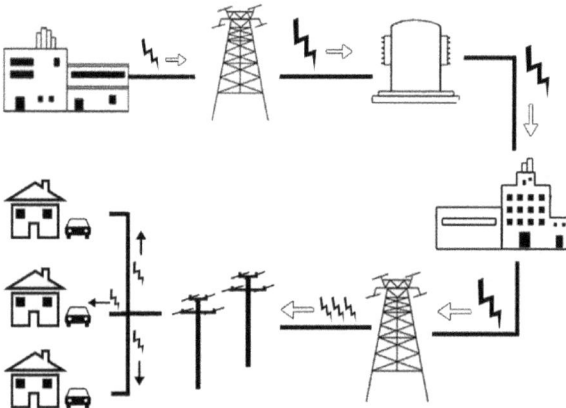

3.10 Electric Grid

POWER CURRENCY

There are three times of loads – base, intermediate, and peak.

Base load plants are coal and nuclear power plants and can operate up to 90 percent of the time. They are very low cost per KWH and are always present. However, at night, they need to shut down some generators, as people are sleeping. These factories are efficient but expensive to build.

Intermediate loads use natural gas and operate 25 to 40 percent of the time. This puts out a lot of power and can ramp up very fast.

Peak load is the cheapest to build and the most expensive to run as they use expensive fuels. These will operate one to ten percent of the time. The cost per KWH can exceed one dollar per KWH.

Engine	Fuel	Capacity	Capacity Factor	Energy Cost
		MW	%	cents/KWH
A	Nuclear	1000	90	2
B	Coal	600	80	3
C	Coal	300	60	4
D	Gas	20	1	12
E	Gas	15	0.5	15
F	Wind	50	20	5
G	Gas	5	0.02	50

3.11 Electricity Load Patterns

Hydropower plants can operate as base or intermediate load. Also, some hydro plants will use power from coal plants to pump water back uphill into the reservoir. This uses the nighttime cheap base load to give potential power for the next day's peak load. A group of plants working to serve a town might look like this.

Electricity by itself will not make a suitable currency. Using Engines, Fuel and Electricity together, we have a system that can support Power Currency. This can compare very well with Gold, Silver and Paper Money.

Accounting Concept	Paper Federal Reserve Notes	Gold and Silver	Power Currency
Assets, Balance Sheet	Long term deposits, Stocks, Bonds	Gold and Silver stored in the Vault	**Engines** that can make the power. Fuels not gathered
Cash Flow, Income Statement	Checking account, cash on hand.	Gold and Silver in the pocket	**Fuels** in the tank ready to be used
Transactions	Cash transacted	Gold and Silver being spent	**Electricity** made, delivered and used

3.12 Power Currency vs Metals and Federal Reserve Notes

Much of the rest of the book deals with moving into a distributed energy system. People make, sell, and broker energy among themselves. There are very powerful interests that are working to use the current money system to transfer wealth from the middle class to a small group of collectivists. Let us take a look at the existing fiat paper money system, the people behind it and the disaster it will bring.

WANKERS

"Give me the power to issue a nation's money; then I do not care who makes the law."

Anselm Rothschild.

"Whoever controls the volume of money in any country is absolute master of all industry and commerce." President James A. Garfield.

Money does not grow on trees – money is made out of thin air by the Federal Reserve Bank.

The Federal Reserve Bank has the most awesome business power - the ability to create money from thin air.   During the course of the last 100 years, they took over the ability to issue money and control nearly one hundred percent of their money in circulation. We will look in further detail how they make money from nothing and charge you interest on this.

The reserve requirement.   In 1913, the reserve requirement demanded that forty percent of all money must be backed by gold. This meant that the banks could create one and a half portions of credit money for each gold dollar it had on hand. At the end of the First World War it was at ten percent. They could create nine dollars of credit money for each gold dollar it had on hand. So there, they gained the ability to make from thin air, more than seven additional dollars and earn interest on that new money. Now, the ratio of gold to money is about one percent, and there is no requirement that the gold be used for reserves. Now, they do not need any gold. Additional money is made based on how much paper money they have in reserves.

There was a steady shift in quality of money also. In 1913, the paper money could be converted to gold and silver. Through a long process, the money was turned into nothing more than paper slips.

Goldfinger:	I prefer to call it an atomic device. It's small, but particularly dirty.
Bond:	Cobalt and iodine?
Goldfinger:	Precisely.
Bond:	Well, if you explode it in Fort Knox, the, uh, entire gold supply of the United States will be radioactive for... fifty-seven years!
Goldfinger:	Fifty-eight, to be exact.
Bond:	I apologize, Goldfinger. It's an inspired deal. They get what they want -- economic chaos in the West -- and the value of your gold increases many times.
Goldfinger:	I conservatively estimate ten times.

The Federal Reserve did not need to use nuclear weapons to destroy the dollar. The destruction of the dollar was carried out in a systematic, planned manner from 1913 until 1965. The mortal gunshot wounds to the dollar were on November 22, 1963.

Until 1963, paper dollars had some degree of promise. There were four parts to the notes –

1. issuing bank

2. amount payable

3. a payee (or bearer)

4. a time for payment (or on demand)

Let's look at the actual words on the United States Notes.

1865-1921, Gold Certificates, secured by gold:

> This certifies that there have been deposited in the Treasury of the United States of America XX Dollars in gold coin repayable to the bearer on demand.

This is pretty good. You can take your dollar bill and you know that it has gold backing with the US Treasury. That is a pretty solid promise.

1922-1933, Gold Certificates, secured by gold:

> This certifies that there have been deposited in the Treasury of the United States of America XX Dollars in gold coin repayable to the bearer on demand. This certificate is a legal tender in the amount thereof in payment of all debts and dues public and private.

1878-1928, Silver Certificates, secured by silver dollars:

> This certifies that there have been deposited in the Treasury of the United States XX silver Dollars payable to the bearer on demand ... This certificate is receivable for customs, taxes and all public dues and when so received may be reissued.

1929-1962, Silver Certificates, secured by silver coin:

> This certifies that there is on deposit in the Treasury of the United States of America XX Dollars in silver payable to the bearer on

demand ... This certificate is a legal tender for all debts public and private.

The early versions of the Federal Reserve Notes were also redeemable in gold and silver on demand at the US Treasury.

1914-1928, Federal Reserve Notes:

The United States of America will pay to the bearer on demand XX Dollars ... This note is receivable by all national and member banks and Federal Reserve Banks and for all taxes, customs and other public dues.

Starting in 1929, the FED added the dreaded 'or other' or the "or other lawful money" clause. So they could give you gold and silver or some other lawful money meaning paper money. Shall we guess which they would choose to give to you?

1929-1933, Federal Reserve Notes:

The United States of America will pay to the bearer on demand XX Dollars ... Redeemable in gold on demand at the United States Treasury, or in gold or lawful money at any Federal Reserve Bank.

1934-1962, Federal Reserve Notes:

This note is legal tender for all debts, public and private, and is redeemable in lawful money at the United States Treasury, or at any Federal Reserve Bank.

JFK planned to issue four billion dollars in new currency that with silver backing. This represented 20 percent of all money in circulation. This money would be debt free with no need to pay the bankers any interest. One week after Kennedy's assassination the first paper notes with no backing came out.

1963 -present, Federal Reserve Notes:

This note is legal tender for all debts, public and private

The end of real money. The paper is the money itself, and you must accept it. It now has no gold or silver backing at all, and no mention of the Treasury or the Federal Reserve Bank.

In 1965 silver backing dropped completely, and in 1968, the old silver certificates were deemed to be only paper, not redeemable in silver. Money now was nothing except for paper. With no constraints the great inflation and debt bubble could begin.

There has always been a struggle for control of money. The USA got this right in the Constitution and Coinage Act of 1792 when they put a penalty of death on those who debase the money. Take a look at Table 1.2 and you see that we are living in an environment where all money is debt based Federal Reserve dollars.

George Washington, Thomas Jefferson, Ben Franklin, and 99 percent of the other patriots who founded our country knew the evils which come from a debt based money system.

> "I sincerely believe that banking institutions are more dangerous to our liberties than standing armies. The issuing power should be taken from the banks and restored to the people to whom it properly belongs."
>
> Thomas Jefferson

> "History records that The Money Changers used every form of abuse, intrigue, deceit, and violent means possible to maintain their control over governments by controlling money, and its issuance."
>
> James Madison

When the States met to draft a Constitution, they decided to standardize the money. Congress would decide on how money was made and measured which would help trade among the States.

In the U.S. Constitution, Article I, Section 8,

> "Congress shall have power to coin money, regulate the value there of"

The Founders knew the evils caused by a fiat currency and looked for a suitable commodity backed money. They chose silver. It was more in use among the population and being more widespread it could not be as easily hoarded, like gold. Silver was considered the people's money; gold was considered the money of the wealthy.

Central Banks were tried in 1781, 1791, and 1816. These all attempted to create money from thin air, and all three banks were killed by Congress. The press of that time attacked the bank and exposed its swindle, the trickery of issuing money from thin air and burdening the taxpayers with debt (similar to today).

This continued through the 19th Century. Lincoln avoided monetary disaster by issuing U.S. Dollars, fiat money called 'Greenbacks'. Still the bankers persisted until they succeeded in gaining control of the money.
The Federal Reserve Act was signed December 23, 1913 giving power to create money to a cartel of private bankers. The Act authorized the establishment of a Federal Reserve Corporation with a Board of Directors to run it. The Act states:

> An Act To provide for the establishment of Federal reserve banks, to furnish an elastic currency, to afford means of rediscounting commercial paper, to establish a more effective supervision of banking in the United States, and for other purposes

The key phrase there is "and for other purposes"
Most people believe the Federal Reserve Banks is a part of government. The FED sure looks like a USA government agency. The name "Federal Reserve" is a clever term to make you think it is an agency of the United States Government. The banks own 100 percent of the Federal Reserve Bank. The Federal Reserve Bank is a private corporation. Our own court

system has ruled on this issue and made it plain and clear. Here are two court cases:

Lewis v. United States, 680 F.2d 1239 (1982)

United States Court of Appeals, Ninth Circuit

Examining the organization and function of the Federal Reserve Banks, and applying the relevant factors, we conclude that the Reserve Banks are not federal instrumentalities for purpose of the FTCA, but are independent, privately owned and locally controlled corporations..... Each Federal Reserve Bank is a separate corporation owned by commercial banks in its region.

Kennedy C. Scott, v. Federal Reserve Bank of Kansas City, et al., (2005)

United States District Court for the Western District of Missouri

Filed: April 28, 2005

The Bank argues that it is not a federal agency for purposes of Rule 4 because Federal Reserve Banks are distinct from the Board of Governors, owned by commercial banks, and directly supervised in their daily operations by separate boards of directors — not the federal government. Further, the Bank states that Federal Reserve Bank employees are not considered federal employees, officials, or representatives for purposes of 12 U.S.C. § 341. The Bank also contends, inter alia, that the plain language of 28 U.S.C. § 451 and relevant case law state that Federal Reserve Banks are not federal agencies.[vii]

The amount of US Government ownership
in the Federal Reserve Banks

0.0 %

Zilch, Nil, Nada, Zip, and Zero.

Zero Point Zero

The ownership of the FED is in proportion to the assets of banks.

> Commercial banks that are members of the Federal Reserve System hold stock in the Reserve Bank in their region, but they do not exercise control over the Reserve Bank or the Federal Reserve System. Holding stock in a regional Reserve Bank does not carry with it the kind of control and financial interest that holding publicly traded stock affords, and the stock may not be sold or traded. Member banks do, however, receive a fixed 6 percent dividend annually on their stock and elect six of the nine members of the Reserve Bank's board of directors.

The shareholders of the Federal Reserve Bank are among thousands of banks, but the concentration of power is in a few hands. Concentration of Assets in the Top four Megabanks is over 40 percent. JP Morgan Chase, Bank of America, Citibank, and Wells Fargo. Concentration of Assets in the Top ten banks is 50 percent. Most of these bankers are Wall Street Bankers - Wankers.

According to the Comptroller of the Currency, the ten largest banks in terms of assets are:

	Assets
JPMORGAN CHASE BANK NA OH	1,627,684,000,000
BANK OF AMERICA NA NC	1,465,221,000,000
CITIBANK NATIONAL ASSN NV	1,161,361,000,000
WELLS FARGO BANK NA SD	1,118,861,000,000
U S BANK NATIONAL ASSN OH	276,376,000,000
PNC BANK NATIONAL ASSN PA	260,310,000,000
HSBC BANK USA NATIONAL ASSN VA	167,165,000,000
SUNTRUST BANK GA	164,341,000,000
BANK OF NEW YORK MELLON NY	164,275,000,000
BRANCH BANKING&TRUST CO NC	159,676,000,000

Average among the other 8002 banks	817,577,131	

Total Assets of all banks	13,107,522,208,000	
Top Four	5,373,127,000,000	41%

Add next six to make Top Ten	6,565,270,000,000	50%
Other 8002	6,542,252,208,000	50%

4.1 Banks by Assets, 2009

You will need to pull the data from multiple sites and put them together.

US Census website

Federal Reserve

Comptroller of the Currency

FDIC

If you take out the top four banks, we see an interesting trend

	Banks	Assets (millions)
2001	9609	643
2010	7755	1,040

From 2001 to 2010, the assets per bank, excluding the top four, grew at about the rate of inflation over ten years – 643 to 1040. However, the number of banks dropped near two thousand. In this same decade, we see a concentration of power moving to the largest four banks. As recently as 2001, the concentration of power in the top five banks was 21 percent. During the decade, the market share doubled. This growth must have been through gobbling up the smaller banks, and legal warfare.

	JPMorgan Chase	Bank of America	Citibank	Wells Fargo/ Wachovia	Market Share
2001	537,826	551,691	452,343	140,675	21%
2002	622,388	565,382	498,676	183,712	26%
2003	628,662	617,962	582,123	250,474	27%
2004	967,365	771,619	694,529	366,256	32%
2005	1,013,985	706,497	1,082,243	403,258	34%
2006	1,179,390	1,196,124	1,019,497	398,671	36%
2007	1,318,888	1,312,794	1,251,715	467,861	38%
2008	1,746,242	1,471,631	1,231,154	538,958	41%
2009	1,627,684	1,465,221	1,161,361	1,118,861	41%
2010	1,568,093	1,518,958	1,157,877	1,073,280	40%

Millions USD

4.1.1 US Banking Cartel by Assets, 2001 - 2010

There is a continuing collectivist trend of the large banks taking over the smaller banks. Give this ten or twenty years and the market share for this Cartel will be well over fifty percent. One way a large bank can do this is to inject a large amount of money into a smaller bank, then that smaller bank will lend out funds. The larger bank then pulls that money out, forcing the smaller bank to call in loans or to crash.

This concentration of power is also reflected in derivatives. The size of the derivatives market is enormous with estimates ranging from 200 trillion to 4000 trillion dollars. According to the Comptroller of the Currency, the amount of Derivatives in the United States is over 200 trillion dollars, and four firms had over ninety percent of this market.

	Trillions	Share
JPMORGAN CHASE	75.5	35.1%
BANK OF AMERICA	44.3	20.6%
CITIBANK	37.5	17.4%
GOLDMAN SACHS	41.6	19.3%
HSBC	2.9	1.3%
WELLS FARGO	4.2	1.9%
BANK OF NEW YORK	1.3	0.6%
All others	8.1	3.7%
Total	215.4	

4.2 Top Derivative traders, Source: US Comptroller

So, between the assets and derivatives, the concentration of financial power is seems to rest with five firms.

You will not see this covered in today's mainstream media. If anyone were to go deep into this issue, they will certainly get some heat or lose their job. Let's look at who is paying them. Consider this when listening to Rush Limbaugh, Bill O'Reilly, Glen Beck, Jim Cramer and others. They will not discuss this issue and if they do, then their career will be hurt. We can see a concentration of Bank Cartel ownership in some of the top media properties.

	DISNEY	TIME WARNER	CBS	General Electric
	ABC	CNN	CBS	NBC
J P MORGAN	5.83%	2.43%	1.30%	8.60%
BANK OF NEW YORK	3.98%	2.23%	2.60%	3.03%
GOLDMAN SACHS	5.10%	0.24%	1.08%	0.77%
WELLS FARGO	2.19%	1.42%	1.59%	1.42%
MORGAN STANLEY	1.56%	0.74%	0.88%	0.52%
BANK OF AMERICA	0.63%	0.85%	1.15%	0.33%

4.3 Bank Cartel ownership in mainstream media

In China, it is taboo to talk about Tiananmen Square, Tibet, Taiwan independence and in America, it is taboo to talk about the ownership of the Federal Reserve Bank. Keep an eye out for this, and see what happens if this topic ever comes up on air. This is even truer now that the US debt has reached into the many trillions.

There are about 1500 institutions that tend to own about seventy percent of these companies. Within the institutional investors, there is a concentration of power. Here is Table 4.4 we see the ownership stakes among very large institutional investors. These manage hundreds of billions of dollars or even trillions of dollars. The issue is the concentration of power and the linkage between the Bank Cartel and major media. These firms collectively own between 23 and 63 percent of these firms. Also, they own all of the stocks in question. If these ten firms decide to do something together – such as the 2008 bailout program – they can do a big power grab financially and in the media. Of course, the executives through the media will say:

> The public own the funds!
> The people's pensions own the funds!
> Conspiracy Nut! There is nothing here!
> Look over there!
> Britney Spears, Lindsay Lohan, Howard Stern!!

Who owns these institutions? If you study this through public sources, you will see that other institutions own each other, banks own the companies that own them, and so forth. It gets difficult to go much deeper and get names. We have to leave it at that and note the concentration of power, the cross ownership, and the control of the media.

In any case, try to find the ownership structure. If Congress can pass laws to wiretap our internet, they can push for detailed information about who the owners of the owners of the owners of the Federal Reserve Bank.

	JP MORGA	Bank of America	Wells Fargo	Citi group	Goldman Sachs	CBS	Disney	General Electric	Time Warner
BLACKROCK	5.40%	4.80%	4.70%	4.80%	5.10%	17.00%	8.00%	9.20%	10.80%
STATE STREET	4.10%	4.50%	3.80%	3.70%	4.00%	9.20%	6.30%	6.70%	7.40%
VANGUARD	7.40%	6.80%	6.20%	6.40%	6.20%	9.50%	5.90%	6.70%	7.30%
FIDELITY	3.30%	1.20%	3.80%	3.20%	1.40%	4.00%	8.20%	3.00%	6.30%
T ROWE PRICE	2.70%	1.00%	1.60%	0.60%	1.30%	0.40%	3.80%	1.80%	8.20%
CAPITAL WORLD	1.40%	1.20%	3.20%	1.70%	3.80%	0.00%	2.30%	2.20%	5.00%
CAPITAL RES. GLOBAL	2.10%	1.40%	1.20%	1.10%	0.00%	2.50%	1.40%	0.90%	10.50%
WELLINGTON MNGT	2.30%	1.30%	2.90%	0.00%	1.60%	6.40%	1.00%	2.30%	2.20%
NORTHERN TRUST	1.30%	1.10%	1.30%	1.00%	1.20%	2.70%	2.40%	2.50%	2.20%
INVESCO	1.20%	0.60%	0.50%	0.50%	0.40%	1.60%	0.50%	1.20%	3.50%
Subtotal	31.10%	23.90%	29.10%	23.10%	25.00%	53.10%	39.80%	36.50%	63.40%

4.4 Cross Ownership of Institutions, Bank Cartel, Major Media

Initially, the Federal Reserve was controlled by a group of banking interests, and now it is controlled by a group of banking interests. Perhaps you can find who controls the large institutions. Maybe the banker bailouts are all a big misunderstanding. All those stories about aggressive foreclosures, and derivatives that kill towns, are all misunderstandings. The owners of these institutions are really such nice people, so nice in fact that they would like to remain anonymous.

Ok, then so what?

The Federal Reserve Notes come from the balance sheet of the Federal Reserve Bank. You can see a simplified balance sheet below. Assets are things like gold and treasury securities, and the liabilities are the amounts owed to shareholder banks, and the Federal Reserve Notes in circulation. Up to 1950, Federal Reserve notes had gold backing to a large degree. From that point on, gold has dropped steadily. The chart below shows that the Federal Reserve notes are about equal to the US Securities.

	Total Assets	Gold	Treas-ury	US Secur-ities	Other	Total Liabil-ities	Bank Reser-ves	Federal Reserve Notes	Other
1950	50	23	5	21	2	49	18	26	6
1960	53	18	5	27	3	52	17	30	5
1970	86	11	7	62	6	85	24	50	11
1980	173	16	14	119	24	172	28	117	28
1990	342	44	20	235	43	330	39	254	47
2000	635	27	32	512	66	629	19	549	61
2009	2267	36	43	777	1412	2241	977	873	391

4.5 Federal Reserve Balance Sheet 1950 to 2009

You can see the huge rise in the balance sheet from 1950 to 2000 and from

2000 to 2009. This reflects the exponential growth of money, and the inflation built into the system.

Notice also that gold declines by half from 1950 to 1970, while the amount of Federal Reserve notes in circulation doubled.

1950 Gold 23 billion; Frollars 26 billion

1960 Gold 18 billion; Frollars 30 billion

1970 Gold 11 billion; Frollars 50 billion

So whereas, in 1950 there was about as many Fed Notes as there was gold, in 1970, this ratio dropped well over 50 percent. This is when the Europeans were started to redeem their Federal Reserve Note dollars into gold and we went off the gold standard. You can see this was a 20 plus year event, and it was not as if Richard Nixon woke up one day in August 1971 and said 'let's not have the dollar linked to gold anymore.'

The Shareholders of the Federal Reserve create money out of thin air, and charge interest on the money that is made out of thin air. This is money that is not backed by gold or silver. It is backed by other money made from thin air. Note that they are charging interest on public resources and your strengths, but they make the money from thin-air invented nothing money. We will see soon that this leads to a transfer of wealth from the private sector over to a small cartel.

Luckily for us, the Chicago Federal Reserve Bank published 'Modern Money Mechanics' in 1968 giving a detailed description of the whole process. The document is no longer online, but you can find it through the search engines.

How this works within the banking system.

1. Bank A creates and lends an amount equal to 90 percent of the reserve requirement.
2. That money is spent into the economy, into another bank. Then 90 percent of that is allowed to be lent out.

3. That money is spent into the economy, into another bank. Then 90 percent of that is allowed to be lent out.

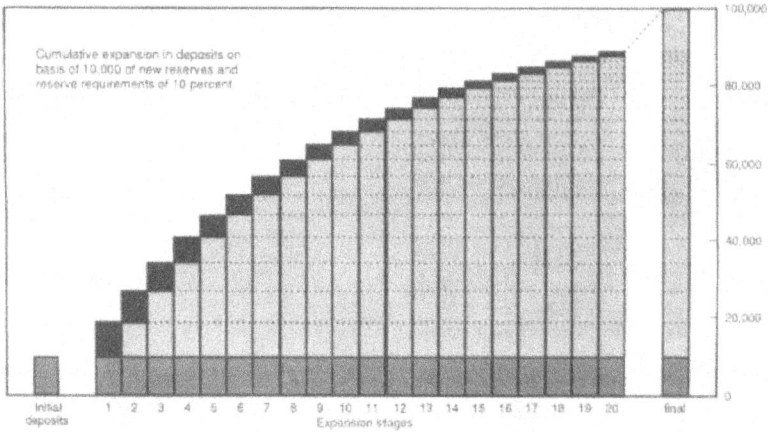

4.6 Fractional Reserve, Money explosion

4. And so on....

Figure 4.6 shows the fractional reserve system with ten percent reserve requirement. Through multiple steps, the money is expanded ten times. The 1,000 dollars can generate 9,000 in lending which must be paid back with interest. Now, the bank is not in itself printing out ten times the money, but the banking system working in cooperation among itself, is able to do this.

If a bank charges for money lent from real assets that is interest earned. They take some risk and provide a service and that interest is good. For money made from nothing we must use the term 'usury'. That money came from nothing and interest comes from money made from nothing.

We showed earlier how there is a lot of cross ownership among the banks, media and institutional investors. Banks can collude to expand money out of thin air. Let's suppose that these banks all want to build some wonderful office buildings. Using fractional reserve banking, they can cooperate to make this happen.

	JPMOR GAN	Bank of America	WELLS FARGO	CITIG ROUP	GOLD MAN SACHS
Percent held by Institutions	74%	60%	77%	58%	73%
	Push Money Through Institutions and Third Parties				
JP MORGAN	/	10%	10%	10%	10%
Bank of America	10%	/	10%	10%	10%
WELLS FARGO	10%	10%	/	10%	10%
CITIGROUP	10%	10%	10%	/	10%
GOLDMAN SACHS	10%	10%	10%	10%	/

4.7 Fractional Reserve Collusion Scenario

All major banks own some shares of other major banks, and we have to assume they have deposits at the other banks. Here is a scenario. Customers, pension funds, and businesses put one billion into these banks. Under fractional reserve, these banks can borrow against this money (900 million at first) and place with other banks in the system. They can take that money and issue out 810 million. Ultimately, they can send this money around among themselves and come up with ten billion dollars out of thin air.

Theoretically, this can go on forever. In a worst case scenario, the Federal Reserve prints money to lend to the government. This goes to the large banks, who then collude to inflate the money supply. With this money made from thin air, they can go to buy industry, farmland, smaller banks and public assets.

Congress can take the power to create currency at any time. It is an awesome privilege and one which the owners of the Federal Reserve do not like to talk about at all!! John F Kennedy was the last one to try to do it and he was shot in the head.

Another example. The New York Federal Reserve Bank buys 100 million USD in US Treasury Bills from a bond dealer with commissions to the dealer. So where does the FED get the 100 million USD? From the tax-payer? No Congress? No. Its vault? No. It creates the money out of thin air. The money gets deposited into an account in a commercial bank - most likely one of the big ones mentioned earlier.

So now we have a net increase of 100 million USD. That bank has 100 million in its account which are used as reserves for that bank. It can use this for loans. The money supply throughout the banking system as a whole increases 1 billion USD.

Using fractional reserve banking, the banks are able to come up with all sorts of new money. These are represented in terms like M1, M2, M3, etc A small percent of the money supply is in actual coin and cash.

- M0 is the coins and currency in people's hands, in the bank or on deposit in the Federal Reserve Banks. Only a small percent of the money supply is in actual currency. In the old days, this was gold and silver. Now it is simply paper money and token coins.
- M1 is the money that circulates in the economy. It includes M0 plus current deposits which people have easy access to spend
- M2 is M1 plus short term deposits in banks up to one year.
- M3 is M2 plus longer term deposits with maturity beyond one year. The Federal Reserve has stopped publishing statistics for this, so you must research and do calculations to find the numbers.
- M4 includes M3 plus foreigner deposits, government deposits
- M?? Stocks, bonds, options, mutual funds, pensions, credit card debt, junk bonds, mortgages, 2nd mortgages, etc
- Mn-2 Futures, Options, Derivatives
- Mn-1 Bundled Derivatives. Gathering of derivatives and betting on certain spreads, and other such.
- Mn Derivatives of bundled derivatives. Bets on derivatives, and other such

	M0	M1	M2	M3	Derivatives
1950	26	108	173	174	
1960	29	140	304	307	
1970	47	209	601	638	
1980	110	396	1,540	1,901	
1990	235	811	3,228	4,124	
2000	523	1,104	4,801	6,839	40,772
2010	887	2,090	8,961	~14,000	236,386

4.8 Credit money explosion, Billions

You can see that the M2 money supply is roughly ten times the M0 money supply. This reflects fractional reserve banking. Here is a comparison of currency inflation, price inflation, and gold prices. You can see a compounded growth rates for gold that tracks very close to the rise in money supply and prices.

	Per Person M0	Per Person M1	Per Person M2	Price Index	Gold Price
1950	169	708	1,134	241	35
1960	159	777	1,684	296	35
1970	230	1,020	2,933	388	35
1980	485	1,738	6,764	824	618
1990	940	3,241	12,906	1,307	383
2000	1,852	3,913	17,014	1,722	279
2010	2,858	6,737	28,885	2,177	1,250
CAGR	4.83%	3.83%	5.54%	3.74%	6.14%

4.9 Credit Money, Prices, Gold, exponential inflation

This reserve requirement is a way to inflate the money system and to transfer power from the free market economy to the usury economy. An entrepreneur gets credit in a normal way. He makes a product and sells for a profit, reinvests that money, and spends into the community. He makes a certain profit margin on his efforts, and needs to borrow against real assets.

It is the system that George Washington, Thomas Jefferson, Abraham Lincoln, Benjamin Franklin, and so many others warned us about. It is the system we have in place now. Unfortunately, our Congressmen in DC, benefit from this system.

REPOCRATS

The only way they can pass this bill is by creating and sustaining a panic atmosphere. … Many of us were told in private conversations that if we voted against this bill on Monday that the sky would fall, the market would drop two or three thousand points the first day and a couple of thousand on the second day, and a few members were even told that there would be martial law in America if we voted no. That's what I call fear fear-mongering, unjustified, proven wrong. We've got a week, we've got two weeks to write a good bill. The only way to write, to pass a bad bill: keep the panic pressure on.

Rep. Brad Sherman (D-CA) on the floor of the House of Representatives. October 2, 2008

Senator James Inhofe stated that Treasury Secretary Henry Paulson was behind the threats of a great depression. Paulson, former Chairman of Goldman Sachs pulled a bait and switch and transferred the money to the large banks. The bailout bill transferred bad debts to the taxpayers while letting the wealthiest banks print money. Since then, the bailout money has gone in secret to some of the largest shareholders of the Federal Reserve Bank.

Most Congressmen do not understand the nature of the debt system. They truly believe there is only one option for money – it must be borrowed into circulation. They do not understand what Lincoln did or how things were done prior to 1913. The Democrats and Republicans may switch power every few years, but the end result is the same. More spending, more taxes, more regulation for the public and a deterioration of the nation's fiscal health. Republicans and Democrats are no different than a single party with two similar factions. We might as well call them the Repocrats. The party platform of the Repocrats:

- Tax and Spend, Spend and Tax
- Foreign wars at our expense
- More regulation
- More debt
- More power to the Federal Government
- More encroachment on the liberties of people.

Repocrats – Republicans and Democrats
Repocrats – Repugnant Autocrats

The talk radio shows like to argue whether it was Republicans or Democrats, Main Street or Wall Street. All the arguments over abortion, gay rights, and such are a diversion from the privately printed fiat money system that is out of control and serving a few masters.

This was not always the case. Ohio Senator, Warren G. Harding, who was elected to the Presidency in 1920, said in a Congressional inquiry, that the Federal Reserve is a private banking monopoly. He said: "The Federal Reserve Bank is an institution owned by the stockholding member banks. The Government has not a dollar's worth of stock in it." His term was cut short in 1923, when he died.

Woodrow Wilson said:

"The growth of the nation ... and all our activities are in the hands of a few men ... We have come to be one of the worst ruled; one of the most completely controlled and dominated governments in the civilized world ... no longer a government of free opinion, no longer a government by conviction and the free vote of the majority, but a government by the opinion and duress of a small group of dominant men."

To give some simple illustration of the relationship, let's look at the Government request to audit financial information.

Congress says to the Federal Reserve. "We want to audit your books to check to see if your information is accurate"
Federal Reserve says to Congress. "No"
Consequences to the Federal Reserve – Trillions in new wealth transferred to their shareholders, huge bonuses for the staff of their shareholding banks

IRS says to You, a US citizen. "We want to audit your books to check to see if your information is accurate"
You say to the IRS. "No"
Consequences to You – jail time, loss of home, wage garnishment, bad credit, loss of access to future opportunities, debt and felony conviction on your records.

Congress can fix this corrupt and evil situation. The final section of the Federal Reserve Act of 1913, Sec. 31, says The right to amend, alter, or repeal this Act is hereby expressly reserved. Congress can abolish the FED or use it for useful purposes.

Many Congressmen and Presidents have seen the fraud in the system. Louis T. McFadden, Chairman of the House Committee on Banking and Currency from 1920-21, accused the Federal Reserve of deliberately causing the Great Depression. In several speeches made shortly after he lost the chairmanship of the Committee, McFadden investigated the Federal Reserve and found it was run by Wall Street banks and their affiliated European banking houses. McFadden said:

> Mr. Chairman, we have in this country one of the most corrupt institutions the world has ever known. I refer to the Federal Reserve Board and the Federal Reserve Banks. The Federal Reserve Board, which is a Government board, has cheated the Government of the United States out of enough money to pay the national debt. The twelve credit monopolies that were deceitfully and disloyally foisted upon this country by the bankers who came here from Europe and repaid us for our hospitality by undermining our American institutions...

There is a way that the Repocrats have transferred the money making authority of Congress over to the Wankers. We will see later that the entire national debt was made from thin air, though the interest on that debt needs to be paid from income taxes. There is a mechanism that the shareholders of the privately owned Federal Reserve are able to make money out of nothing, and then charge interest to the taxpayers?

Whenever the Congress is short of money it turns to the Federal Reserve and use the following steps whereby government debt is funded.

"Step 1. Pass a higher debt limit so that they can borrow more money. Congress can issue interest free Government bonds, or issue more money, but they will borrow instead.

Step 2. Write up an interest bearing bond for the money it needs. Sell it to the Federal Reserve

Step 3. The Federal Reserve will buy it and charge interest on it.

Step 4. The US Treasury writes checks against this money.

Step 5. The recipients of the checks will spend the money and most of it will land in a bank.

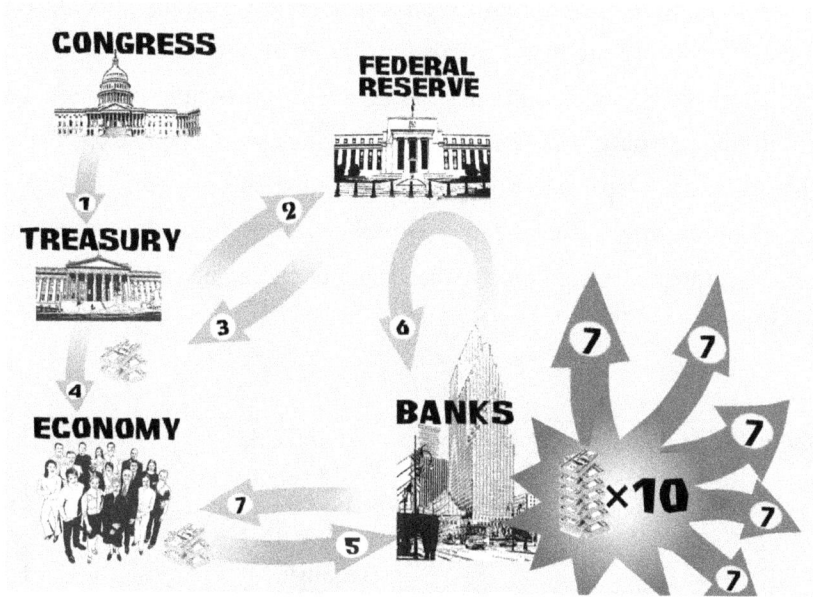

5.1 Debt and money creation process

Step 6. New bank sends this money back to the Federal Reserve. The Federal Reserve receives it and increases the reserve account by that amount. Now the reserve requirement is about ten percent.

Step 7. The bank can lend out 90 percent of that, but the ultimate effect is the banking system can increase the amount in circulation by about ten times.

Note that all this new money is made from nothing, but the banks get to charge interest on it. This would make Satan envious. With this mechanism in place it is easier to see how and why the housing bubble was pushed so hard to expand. The money is invented from nothing, and when the bubble pops, the bank can come in and take the home, land and property of the borrowers. If the large banks can cooperate to make the thin-air money, then when the housing bubble pops, they can write down the money but still get to push people for full payment on loans.

In step seven above, the multiplication effect done through fractional reserve banking allows the banks to create trillions of new dollars from thin air. So every dollar created through government borrowing, becomes ten dollars in the economy. The key is that the banks work together to make this happen and the top banks do work to manipulate the system.

Congress can simply issue the money debt free to build infrastructure projects. As the projects complete, then the money can be retired. Here is a comparison.

USURY SYSTEM	Debt	AMERICAN SYSTEM	Debt
Debt through Shareholders of the Federal Reserve **Government needs 30 million dollars**		National Credit issued by the US Treasury **Government needs 30 million dollars**	
Goes to the Federal Reserve bank and asks for the money. Then the Bank asks the US Treasury to print the money. Then the Treasury prints the money and gives to the Bank. Then the bank will lend back to the Government at 4 % interest over 30 years. Then the Government pays 30 million principal and 36 million interest for 30 years until it is paid off.	**36 Million**	The Government issues the money. Government backs money production from the project. Keeps money in circulation	**Zero**

Usury Way		Lincoln Way	
Government needs 345 million dollars		Government needs 345 million dollars	
Goes to Wall Street and asks for the money.	**Billions**	The Government issues the money backed by national wealth. Keeps money in circulation until Federal Reserve retires the notes in the 1990's	**No** **Debt**

Federal Reserve Way		Kennedy Way	
United States needs Funds to pay the deficit.		United States needs 400 million.	
Then the Bank asks the treasury to print the money. Then the Treasury prints the money and gives to the Bank.		The Treasury issues the money backed by silver.	**Zero** **Debt**
Federal Reserve buys a portion of this debt at 2%. Member Banks will issue new money through fractional reserve, and buy debt at 5%. Then the bank will lend back to the Government at 5 % interest over 30 years. Exponential growth in debt.	**Trillions**	Kennedy gets two bullets in the head. Silver Certificates confiscated by Federal Reserve Bank and replaced by debt based Federal Reserve Notes	

5.2 Usury vs American System

But the Repocrats want to do more than tax you. They want to go after your freedoms and rights. In our own Congress there are pending bills which would create strict rules, fines, inspections, and onerous bureaucracies that can only be described as tyranny. For example, in the energy legislations, the Federal Government will:

> Mandate a 70 percent reduction of energy phased in over the next 20 years.

> Take away the States power to set building codes

> Enforce with fees, penalties, and mandates

> Monitor individual energy use

> Set up a framework of fees and penalties for non-compliance.

> Mandate the use of smart appliances

> The smart appliances will collect individual information and send to remote sites

> Sets up a new Army of inspectors and police to inspect and enforce the law.

> The new inspectors will have the right to enter your home or business for this purpose

> The Secretary of Energy will have freedom to change this law (make it even worse) as long as he is acting in the implied intent of the law.

> What is the implied intent? Is there any limit here?

This opens up opportunities for intrusive monitoring and control.

Here is an example of the law. Go read for yourself. This 1428 page bill is full of onerous rules and regulations. Go to this link

http://www.gpo.gov/fdsys/pkg/BILLS-111hr2454eh/pdf/BILLS-111hr2454eh.pdf

And to start you can read the Second and Third Section.

H.R. 2454: American Clean Energy and Security Act of 2009
TITLE II—ENERGY EFFICIENCY

2 Subtitle A—Building Energy
3 Efficiency Programs

Here is one of the sections, to give you a feel for the law. It talks about States which fail to comply.

"(C) NONCOMPLIANCE.—Any State that is not in compliance with this section, as provided in subparagraph (A), shall, until the State regains such compliance, be ineligible to receive—

"(i) emission allowances pursuant to subsection (h)(1);

"(ii) Federal funding in excess of that State's share (calculated according to the allocation formula in section 363 of the Energy Policy and Conservation Act (42 U.S.C. 6323)) of $125,000,000 each year; and

"(iii) for—

"(I) the first year for which the State is out of compliance, 25 percent of any additional funding or other items of monetary value otherwise provided under the American Clean Energy and Security Act of 2009;

"(II) the second year for which the State is out of compliance, 50 percent of any additional funding or other items of monetary value otherwise provided under the American Clean Energy and Security Act of 2009;

"(III) the third year for which the State is out of compliance, 75 percent of any additional funding or other items of monetary value otherwise provided under the American Clean Energy and Security Act of 2009; and

"(IV) the fourth and subsequent years for which the State is out of compliance, 100 percent of any additional funding or other items of monetary value otherwise provided under the American Clean Energy and Security Act of 2009.

Note that first the law will take money for the citizens of that State, and then will withhold that money from the State if they do not comply. There are no ifs, ands or buts about it.

Repocrats have no sense of future technologies - 3D television, 100 inch flat screens, hologram NFL sports in your well lit energized family room. What about the indoor hot tubs, wonderful gadgets, extensive lighting systems, wonderful cooking appliances?

When I showed portions of this law to students in China, they were amazed. They could not believe the USA could write such a bill. To them it was a throwback to the stories from their parents about the Cultural Revolution - inspections, entering homes, gathering data, enforcing regulations, neighbors snitching on neighbors.

This law passed the House of Representatives, and except for a few votes in the Senate, would be law now.

Ok, so what! Things are bad, but they are not that bad.
Let's go onto where all this is leading if we allow the fiat money system to evolve much further.

SLAVERY 2.0

As a military general would look at a map and find the situation and plot strategy, collectivists look at the Flow of Funds to find opportunities to shift huge portions of the economy from one side to the other. The Federal Reserve Bank published the flow of funds report each quarter. This report gives a snapshot of the condition of the national economy.

This is a steady progression of more and more debt, slowly and over time. There is no up and down short term trend. The trend is constant and in one direction. This reflects the mathematical nature of the debt, and the 100 percent control over the money that the Federal Reserve enjoys. The net effect is just a few percent per year, but the long term results are horror. Assets are stripped away from the USA economy and moved over into the financial sector and offshore accounts controlled by hedge funds, private equity, old money, foreign dictators, and other such types.

Here is a breakdown of the Net Assets positions of the various sectors in the flow of funds from 1952 to 2010. Anything below the line is in debt, and above the line positive assets.

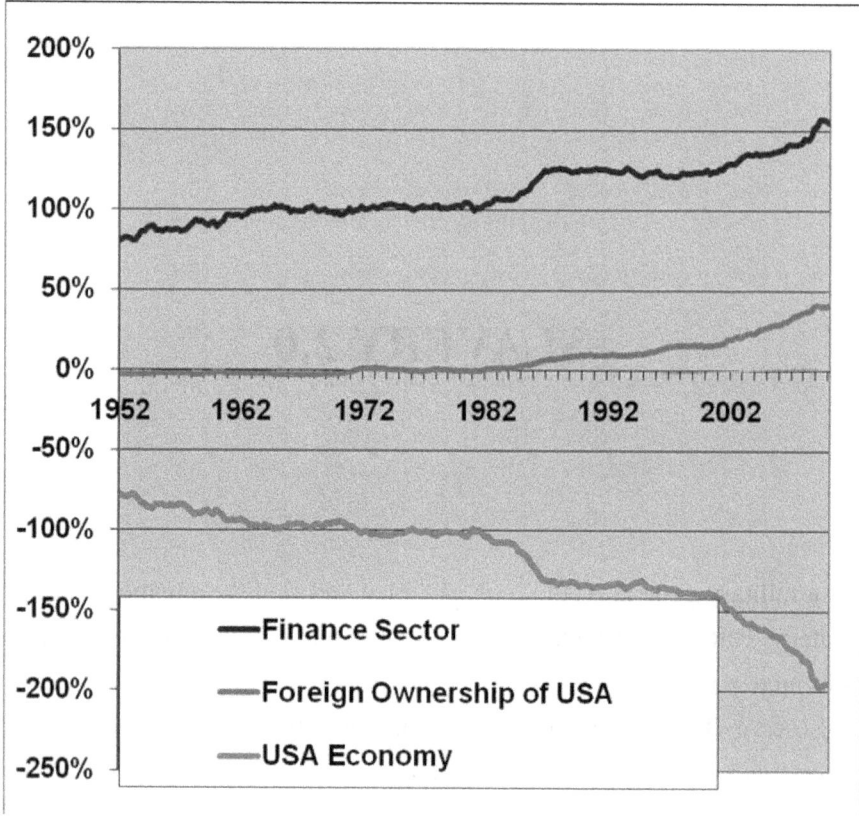

6.1 Shift in assets Source: Flow of Funds, United States

USA Economy = Finance Sector + Foreign Ownership of USA

The scale on the left is the amount compared to the GDP. The two lines at the top show the growth in the financial sector and shows the assets taken by foreigners in relation to the USA GDP. The line at the bottom shows the increasing debt load of the total US economy.

Domestic nonfinancial sectors credit market consists of five parts:

Federal Government

State and Local Government

Households – that's all of us

Nonfarm nonfinancial corporate – Walmart, Ford, small stores, etc

Nonfarm noncorporate – churches, schools, etc

Until the mid 1980's we were carrying a total debt about equal to our GDP, though there was a steady trend downward. Since that time, and especially since 2001, the rise in debt has been quickening.

Based on Figure 6.1, here are three projections for our debt to GDP levels in the future. The best case scenario has it reaching 280 percent of GDP. This cannot be avoided through raising taxes. It is a mathematical certainty because all of our money is issued as debt and that debt needs to be paid back to the banking cartel.

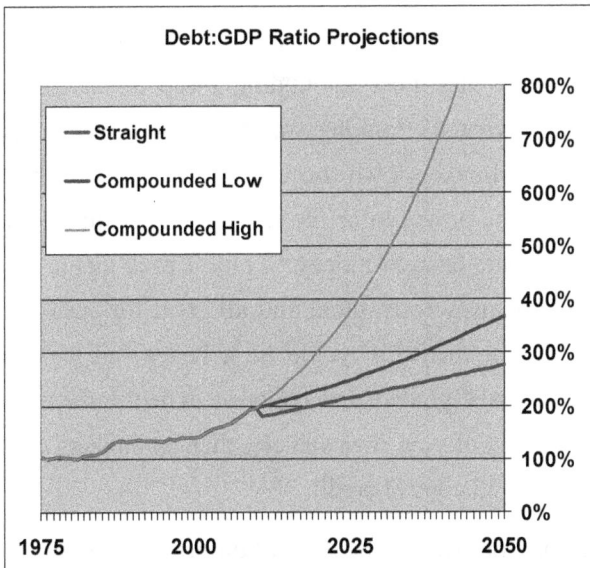

6.2 GDP/Debt projections

If we take the growth rate from the past ten years, the debt to GDP will be over ONE THOUSAND percent by 2050. At that point, the country is completely different. It will be debt slavery for 99 percent of the people serving one percent at the top. This brings us back to Medieval Europe. Those one percent usurers certainly want this to happen.

The banking cartel makes hundreds of billions in profit through legal manipulation and loaning money that is made from thin air. This collection of interest from money backed by nothing is usury. Usury has a long history dating back thousands of years. The usury system is the most profitable system ever invented – if you are the debt collector. It is a massive drain on the economy and a transfer of wealth from the production part of the economy over to the bank cartel.

From time to time, some of them will have a conscience or will boast. Sir Josiah Stamp, president of the Bank of England and the second richest man in Britain in the 1920s declared in an address at the University of Texas in 1927:

> "The modern banking system manufactures money out of nothing. The process is perhaps the most astounding piece of sleight of hand that was ever invented. Banking was conceived in inequity and born in sin . . . . Bankers own the earth. Take it away from them but leave them the power to create money, and, with a flick of a pen, they will create enough money to buy it back again. . . . Take this great power away from them and all great fortunes like mine will disappear, for then this would be a better and happier world to live in. . . . But, if you want to continue to be the slaves of bankers and pay the cost of your own slavery, then let bankers continue to create money and control credit."[viii]

A company like Ford Motor Company made 2.7 billion profit in 2009. To do this they had to employ 159,000 people. They had to engineer, design, promote, market, build, and do all the functions. They have to have hundreds of factories, finance the land, build, and maintain the buildings and equipment. For large financial institutions, hundreds of billions can be

taken through legalizing usury systems and private issuance of money.
There are various collectivists systems to study – China's Cultural Revolution, Nazi Germany, Stalin's purges. The tricky ones are the slow to develop. The termites destroy homes just as effectively as fire, but they take a long time. Now, the collectivism that is happening is a few percent a year. With the recent recession, it is becoming more open. We need to be aware of the slow collectivism, and guard against it. Here is a comparison.

Freedom	Collectivist	
Distributed Private sector production based	Centralized National system	Centralized Debt based usury system
Republic	Kings, Dictators	Feudal Lords, Usurers
Washington	Stalin, Hitler, Mao	Rockefeller, Scrooge
People, States	Strong Central Government	Federal Reserve,
Limited Debt	People in debt to Party	People in debt to system
Gold, Silver, other types	Government Fiat Paper Money	Federal Reserve Dollars
Free Market	Communists, Nazis, Fascists	Debt Slavery, Feudalism

6.3 Collectivism and Freedom

We are moving from the private sector system over to the Collectivist systems. Here is how I see the Path to Slavery 2.0

1. Gain control over the Government debt and money system.
2. Set up the mechanism to transfer real wealth.
3. Increase spending and debt exponentially.   Weaken the Middle Class

4. Destroy liberties and property rights.
5. Collect on the debt. Seize lands, homes, assets, mineral rights, public utilities and public lands. Demonize dissent. Kill opponents. Tyranny.

Gain control over the money system.

Every collectivist will do this. Mao did it immediately; Hitler nationalized the money system. Collectivists in the USA have done this through the Federal Reserve Bank, legal mechanisms, fractional reserve collusion, and strict control over access to money.

Set up mechanisms to transfer real wealth.

Why do things seem to be so bad in America today? Unemployment is the worst in decades, debt levels are off the chart, war is constant and our standing in the world is falling off a cliff. Many who do have jobs are settling for lower wages and benefits. Why are countries like China copying our technology and taking control of markets all over the world. Why are our students taking on huge debt loads, and can't find a decent job when they graduate? People are losing their pensions, our States are losing their wealth, and our neighbors are losing their homes. Unlike past recessions, we have lost our manufacturing base, are deep in debt, and face a far more competitive environment in the world. Much of this destruction in national wealth has happened in just the past ten to twenty years. There are a number of ways the wealth transfer has taken place.

- Transfer or wealth out of America through trade imbalances
- Transfer well paying jobs to other countries.
- Taxation that targets the middle class.
- Boom and busts cycles by design
- Constant Wars
- Usury interest payments on money made from thin air.

Trade Deficits

The United States has given up its role as the producer of the world. The US trade balance exceeded 700 billion dollars in 2008. When NAFTA was passed in the 1990's, the Clinton Administration stated that all the extra exports would generate jobs[ix]. Since that time, a great deal of our manufacturing base has gone offshore, and unemployment has soared. This experiment with globalization is a great success for the globalists. It is a disaster for the middle class.

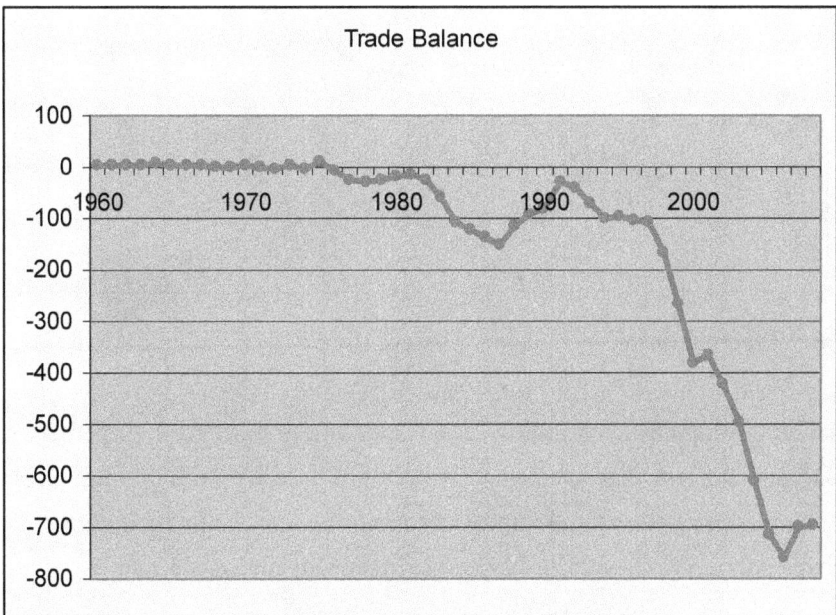

Trade Balance

6.4 Trade Balance   Source: US Census

US oil imports are the largest component of the trade deficit. Until recently, we were energy independent, but now we import 60 percent of our oil. Every time someone fills up their gas tank, much of that money leaves the community and goes overseas. Since the attacks on September 11, 2001, we have sent more money to OPEC for crude oil than in all the time from 1900 to 2001. Any way to make our own fuel will help the economy.

The USA has lost its edge in manufacturing. In the 1940's and 1950's manufacturing accounted for close to 30 percent of our GDP and was over twice as large as the financial sector. We were the factory of the world and this helped support a strong middle class.

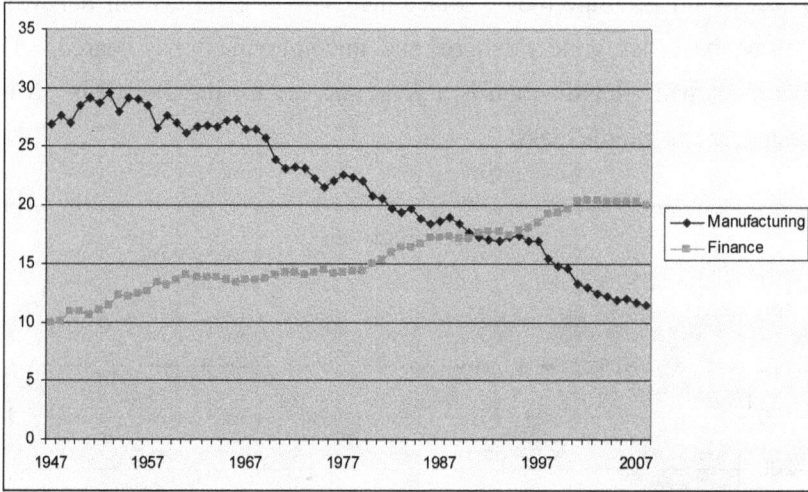

6.5 Manufacturing vs Finance Source: Bureau of Economic Analysis

Manufacturing has been hollowed out and is little more than 10 percent of GDP and far less than the financial sector. While we rack up huge debts, we shift jobs overseas and import cheap goods, much of which is made in conditions we find morally bankrupt. You will notice we had a positive balance in trade into the 1970s's.

Taxation

Let's look at the taxation in America. Today we accept as a rule that the income tax is the primary means to raise taxes for government services. About 80 percent of tax revenue in 2009 is from your wages. Twenty percent comes from all other sources - corporate income, excise taxes on fuel, alcohol, cigarettes, and customs duties on imports. If you go onto the Census Bureau or Whitehouse websites and download data regarding taxes, you find the data goes back only to about 1934 when the Social Security system started. The total tax receipts go back to 1792, but the details by source go back to 1934. To go further back, you will need to download old Statistical Abstracts from the Census site, and then look up the numbers in the PDF file. In the early days, most taxes were collected in tariffs and excise taxes. The tariffs were a good revenue generator and protected the American worker from cheap products that were being produced in India. It worked very well to protect jobs, build manufacturing and help everyone have a decent livable wage. Later there were a number of tariffs tied to alcohol, tobacco, and other items. In 1916 about the same time as the passing of the Federal Reserve, we see the income tax come. Here is the change in taxes during the 20th Century.

	1900	1950	2000
Customs Revenue	**35%**	**1%**	**1%**
Alcohol	26%	6%	0%
Tobacco	9%	3%	0%
Transportation	0%	0%	2%
Other Excise	0%	10%	0%
Taxes on Companies	8%	26%	10%
Postal Service Revenue	15%	0%	0%
Financial and Miscellaneous	6%	1%	2%
Individual Income and SSA	**0%**	**51%**	**82%**
Estate and Gift Taxes	0%	2%	1%

6.6 Taxes – 20th Century Shift

Step by step the revenue shifted to an income tax. You will notice that the tax debate is always about over who pays the share of income taxes. The tax debates never bring up levying customs duties again, or taxing imported oil. You also see a significant portion of the revenue around 1900 came from postal service revenue. We will address how to set up a system where a large chunk of revenue for governments comes from energy production. In other countries there are taxes on financial transactions, on home sales, stock transactions and import tariffs. Repocrats will not discuss this. All Repocrats agree that taxes must come from income first and foremost.

The Shareholders of the Federal Reserve create boom and busts cycles. They know beforehand when the booms and busts will come, and they profit from that inside knowledge. To create a boom, all the Federal Reserve board needs to do is to lower the interest rates and relax the reserve requirements.

1993 - 2000 Stock market boom

2001 – 2006 Real estate boom

2008 – ongoing – thin air money boom

Then to create the bust, they can make changes the other way.

2001 Nasdaq bust

2007 – ongoing. Real estate deflation

1980 – 1982 recession.

The question for you is simple. Do the shareholders of the Federal Reserve and their friends have inside information about what is coming in the future? If they do, then it is very easy to make money whichever direction the market takes.

Increase spending and debt exponentially.

The more debt they can build with as much waste as possible. This is the recipe collectivists desire. The best method is a long protracted war against an enemy that cannot fight back with nuclear weapons. The national debt is growing hundreds of billions each year, with no end in sight. Since 1963 there has been an explosion of debt.

During the 1800's, the national debt was just a few dollars per person.

This stayed reasonable until recently. You can see in the figure below how this has grown dramatically and is doubling each decade. Factoring in population growth and inflation, the debt is still awful. We will discuss later, how this trend cannot reverse.

	Debt per person
1800	16
1810	7
1820	9
1830	4
1840	0
1850	3
1860	2
1870	64
1880	42
1890	25
1900	28
1910	29
1920	245
1930	131
1940	325
1950	1701
1960	1597
1970	1824
1980	4007
1990	13000
2000	20094
2010	42258

6.7 Debt per person

Lets put this into perspective. After World War One, Germany had to pay reparations. They were worn out from the War, the blockade, and flu pandemic. They signed the treaty which compelled them to pay an enormous

amount of money - 31.4 billion dollars, payable in gold.   This led to severe depression, monetary collapse and the rise of Hitler.   Taking into
account the population (about 60 million) and the change in value of gold
(1200 dollars in 2010), this amounts to less than 30,000 dollars per person
in 2010 money. So, the debt load they had to pay which led to great misery,
was far less than the amount that every American man, woman and child
has to pay to cover the U.S. national debt. This US debt was made from
thin air.

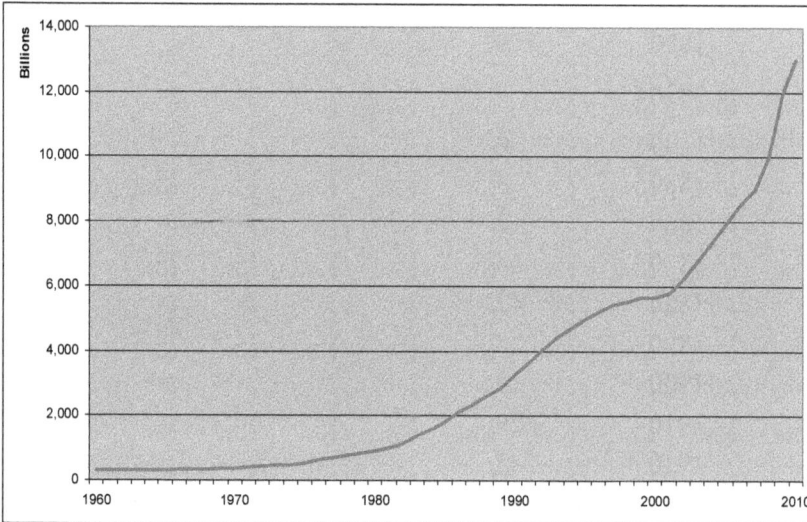

6.8 National Debt Source: US Census

It gets worse as we look at obligations in the future. Social Security, Medicare and other entitlements guarantee we will extend this burden until we
die. If you take into account Social Security and Medicare obligations as
well as personal, state, and unfunded pensions, the amount is over 200,000
dollars per person.

Now we are above 14 trillion in debt, and the interest rates are low. Just
wait until the interest rates start to move up. Debt payments drain more
than four percent of the economy each year. This is a severe drag on the
economy, makes us less competitive, and works its way into the price of

goods and services.   Worse still is the outlook for the future. The debt will grow faster and faster. It compounds, and accelerates. There really is no way to pay off the debt.

This is a mathematical phenomenon. It is useless to talk about raising taxes and cutting spending at this point. No matter what we do to try to pay off this debt, it will grow. On the one hand this could be a reason for despair. On the other hand it is a reason for optimism. We can find a solution to this problem and bring the people to justice.

Here below is the national debt and a best fit exponential curve of 6.8 percent.

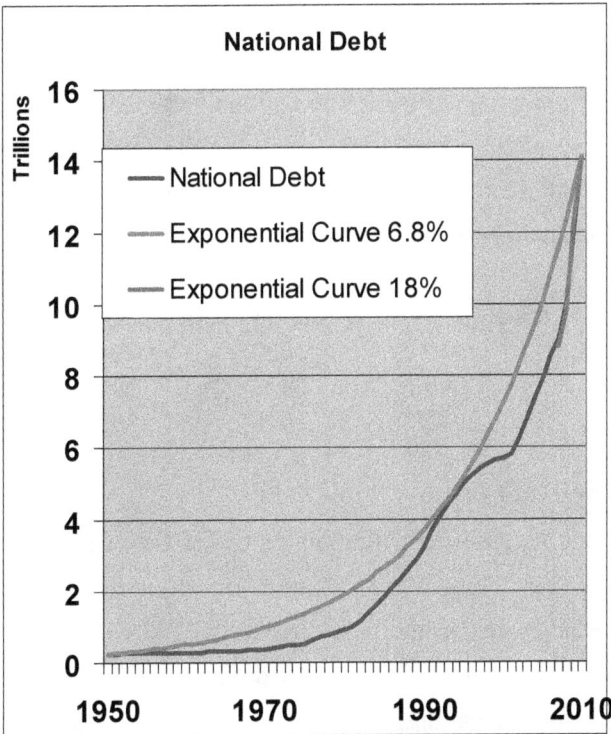

National Debt

6.8 Exponential Debt

Not only is the national debt growing but it is accelerating. It is as if you are in a runaway car, with no breaks, and pedal to the metal.

The growth rate itself is getting larger.

     1950's and 1960's one to two percent

     1970's through 1990's three to eight percent

     2000 to 2007 ten to twelve percent

     2008 to 2010 fifteen to eighteen percent

     2010 to 2020   faster??

To turn this around, our Congress decides to collect more taxes, which takes more money out of the producers and further depresses the economy. For those collecting social security, future payments are in doubt.

Can younger people believe there will be a Social Security system in place when they retire? Would you say 50 trillion in national debt is too much? Would 100 trillion be too much? Would ONE THOUSAND TRILLION be too much? Here are the projections at 6.8 percent 12 percent and 18 percent growth rates, and which year we will hit those amounts.

Future Debt Level	6.8 percent	12 percent	**18 percent**
50 Trillion	2030	2022	**2018**
100 Trillion	2040	2028	**2022**
1000 Trillion	2075	2048	**2036**

    6.10 Future Debt Projections

In 1960, people could not imagine one trillion in debt. The debt was growing about one percent a year. Now, we can imagine one thousand trillion. At the growth rate we have seen in the past three years, we will see our national debt pass ONE THOUSAND TRILLION dollars in 2036. At that point, the word 'dollar' has no meaning.

We must realize this debt is a product of legal mechanisms, and replacement of the United States Dollars with Federal Reserve Dollars. We either fix this mechanism, or we move into Debt Slavery.

War and Debt

One of the key drivers of debt growth is war. During times of peace, the debt levels have not increased much at all. In fact, taking into account the rise in population, the per person debt levels would decrease. Average increase in debt each year in peacetime:

Peacetime	1865 - 1914	0%
	1919 - 1941	3%
	1945 - 1971	2%

War is good for the debt creation business. Let's look at the average annual increase in debt during times of war:

Civil War	1861 - 1865	133%
1st World War	1914 - 1919	57%
2nd World War	1941 - 1945	52%

6.11 War and National Debt

The annual compounded increase is phenomenal if you are the lender. During the Civil War, the amount lent by banks was backed by silver and gold. During the First and Second World War, the money lent was backed by gold and credit. Now, the money is generated from thin air but interest is paid from taxes that comes from people's hard earned money.

During the fiat money time, debt levels boom as the money is issued out of thin air. Average increase in debt each year during Federal Reserve Dollar only period:

100 percent Federal Reserve Dollars	1971 - 2009	10%

Since 1971, we have seen over 97 percent of the rise in our debt. In fact, under an honest money system, and with the technology we have developed, there would be no national debt now if not for the unsound money system.

Do we believe other countries will peacefully and dutifully continue to buy trillions of dollars of our debt. Throughout history, countries that swim in debt will eventually collapse

The total accumulated interest payments on the national debt are about equal to the debt itself. If the money had been issued by Congress as it was prior to 1914, then we would have no national debt and no interest payments on that debt each year. This is a scam and is a wealth transfer mechanism. In 2001, the accumulated interest paid was more than the national debt. Now it is almost as much. We are just rolling over the interest year after year. The national debt is not because of greediness on the part of the population. It is not caused by illegal immigrants, social security, Medicare or even defense spending. It is a mathematical and legal construction 100 percent guaranteed to happen. The amazing thing is that the larger our economy becomes, the bigger the debt we will have.

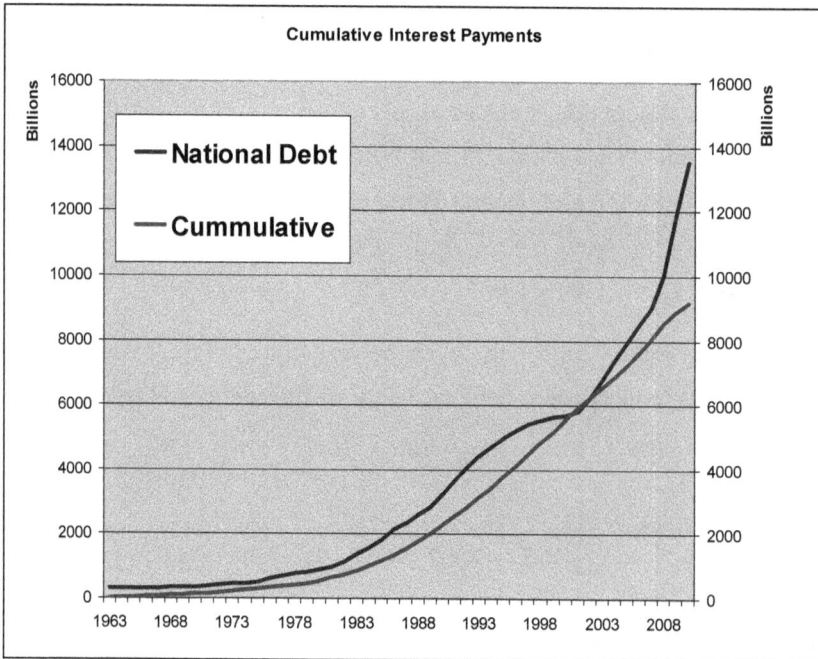

6.12   National Debt Scam

This is the biggest scam in all of history. The primary factor driving this is the inflated money supply. Even if we used all of the money we have in our economy, we could not pay off the national debt.

Destroy liberties.

No matter how bad things get, if we have our liberties, we will be ok in the end. The Collectivists must go after guns, privacy, private property, and other liberties. The Nazis and Red Guards did this by turning neighbor against neighbor. They also do this by controlling access to money, and creating a series of obstacles and regulations to destroy liberty.

It is a psychological operations technique to box people in and make them feel helpless and fearful.

- There was never any other money except for the money we control
- You must do this, or else something terrible will happen
- The economy will recover if you vote for....

The Bill of Rights was set up to guard against tyranny. Now, we see this in the whole range of new laws and executive orders. The Patriot Act, wire tapping, TSA, and so forth. The Collectivists will also go after physical property and intellectual property rights.

Print Money. Take the money and use it to buy real assets.

Since 2008, we start to see the End Game. With large deficits, start to transfer assets from the middle class over to the collectivists. Then through force of law, force the debtor to put up real assets for the money you create from nothing. The final chapter will lead to collectivist seizing public lands, homes, assets, mineral rights, public utilities and everything else they can. Once this happens, then true tyranny will take place. They will demonize opposition and kill 'enemy's of the people/state' for 'the public good'.

To illustrate some of the current transfers. Here is the profits that the banking cartel made through derivatives.

Year	Millions$		
1995	6,137	Win	Bankers keep this
1996	7,495	Win	Bankers keep this
1997	8,006	Win	Bankers keep this
1998	7,903	Win	Bankers keep this
1999	10,376	Win	Bankers keep this
2000	12,392	Win	Bankers keep this
2001	12,890	Win	Bankers keep this
2002	10,727	Win	Bankers keep this
2003	11,369	Win	Bankers keep this
2004	9,874	Win	Bankers keep this
2005	14,385	Win	Bankers keep this
2006	18,787	Win	Bankers keep this
2007	5,489	Win	Bankers keep this
2008Q1	721	Win	Bankers keep this
2008Q2	1,614	Win	Bankers keep this
2008Q3	6,005	Win	Bankers keep this
2008Q4	**(-9176)**	**LOSS**	**TAXPAYER PAYS THIS**
2009Q1	9,768	Win	Bankers keep this
2009Q2	5,172	Win	Bankers keep this
2009Q3	5,720	Win	Bankers keep this
2009Q4	1,932	Win	Bankers keep this
2010Q1	8,263	Win	Bankers keep this
2010Q2	6,600	Win	Bankers keep this

6.13 Wankers Scam, Gambler's dream

Between 1995 and 2010, the total revenue from derivative trades was 172 Billion dollars. Nearly all revenue is profit. Derivatives are very high profit margin ventures with no real cost for materials or labor. If the derivative traders had taken the loss, their revenues would be 172 billion. With the taxpayer bailout, the figure is over 200 billion, and perhaps far more, when you consider all the low interest loans from the Federal Reserve.

Summarized in figure 6.16 are our oil imports, Federal Government debt, cumulative trade deficit, and net assets. How much longer can this go on?

Will this trend reverse, level off, continue rising or speed into hyperinflation? Here is a summary of the national loss of wealth. All of this was done through legal mechanisms, printing money from thin air and charging interest on that money.

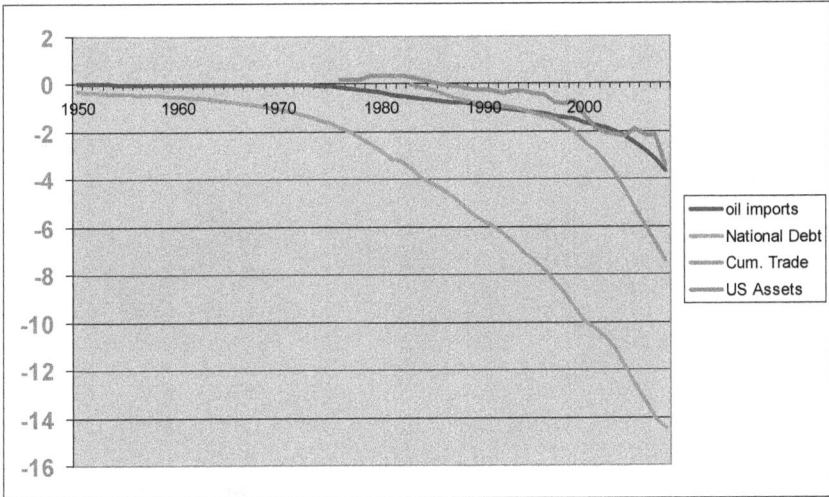

6.14 USA Loss of Wealth in Trillion Dollars

Source: Census, Flow of Funds, Bureau of Economic Analysis

Up to now, we have lost out to an organized banking cartel that knows exactly what it wants and has a plan to get it. This is the essence of collectivism. They gather up your resources and put them into a central pot that they control.

We will move into a discussion of the Smart Grid and then look at remedies for this situation. The solution is available, and we are 95 percent there.

SMART SURVEILLANCE GRID

Can you imagine using the old telephone system with copper wires? Most of the country is served by an electric grid build decades ago.

The Internet replaced the old telephone network and we will see more of the same now with distributed energy. Software and telecom enable a lot of the new capabilities.

It is conceivable that we could triple our energy production without needing to add too much in the way of high voltage transmission lines. The utilities may need to upgrade their transformers and such equipment as new power sources come online. In a modern network, the computers communicate automatically to link with compatible partners.

The power grid has capacity constraints are aging and expensive to improve. Construction of new power plants and transmission capacity is expensive. At times, demand for electricity has caused shortages, brown outs, and occasional large scale blackouts. Utilities and software companies build their networks to meet customer demand. The conventional way to handle customer demand is to build more power plants, which requires a large amount of capital and planning. This book proposes that while some large power plants are fine, it is not necessary. The power developed through distributed energy could easily triple the output by 2030 without any new large power plants. The smart grid takes the IT tools we use, and applies it to the antiquated electricity grid.

The demand side programs in place push consumers to change their energy use through efficiency and load management.

The Department of Energy defines the Smart Grid:

- Intelligent – capable of sensing system overloads and rerouting power to prevent or minimize a potential outage; of working autonomously when conditions require resolution faster than humans can respond…and cooperatively in aligning the goals of utilities, consumers and regulators

- Efficient – capable of meeting increased consumer demand without adding infrastructure

- Accommodating – accepting energy from most fuel sources including solar and wind as easily and transparently as coal and natural gas; capable of integrating any and all better ideas and technologies – energy storage technologies, for example – as they are market-proven and ready to come online

- Motivating – enabling real-time communication between the consumer and utility so consumers can tailor their energy consumption based on individual preferences, like price and/or environmental concerns

- Opportunistic – creating new opportunities and markets by means of its ability to capitalize on plug-and-play innovation wherever and whenever appropriate

- Quality-focused – capable of delivering the power quality necessary – free of sags, spikes, disturbances and interruptions – to power our increasingly digital economy and the data centers, computers and electronics necessary to make it run

- Resilient – increasingly resistant to attack and natural disasters as it becomes more decentralized and reinforced with Smart Grid security protocols

- "Green" – slowing the advance of global climate change and offering a genuine path toward significant environmental improvement

DOE lists five fundamental technologies that will drive the Smart Grid:

- Integrated communications, connecting components to open architecture for real-time information and control, allowing every part of the grid to both 'talk' and 'listen'
- Sensing and measurement technologies, to support faster and more accurate response such as remote monitoring, time-of-use pricing and demand-side management
- Advanced components, to apply the latest research in superconductivity, storage, power electronics and diagnostics
- Advanced control methods, to monitor essential components, enabling rapid diagnosis and precise solutions appropriate to any event
- Improved interfaces and decision support, to amplify human decision-making, transforming grid operators and managers quite literally into visionaries when it come to seeing into their systems

Many people compare the transformation of the smart grid to the building of the interstate highway system. That is a good analogy if you are a big utility and looking to such up infrastructure spending.

The smart grid has the potential to be good or bad. Utilities and governments could collect trillions of bits of information and compile dossiers on our personal lives. The potential for abuse is enough the make a Stasi agent in old East Germany jump for joy. What will the companies and government do with the data? If they will not use it to control people, then why collect it in the first place?

Bad Smart Grid	Good Smart Grid
Collectivism and Control	**Freedom**
Customer must share data under force of law	Customer is free to share data
Penalties if do not share	No penalties
No privacy	Privacy
All residents must allow agents into home	4th Amendment is honored
Must go through a central hub.	Peer to Peer Electricity. Free to have direct contact with others
Mandatory meter in home to collect data	Meter is optional
Shut down appliances during peak load and no compensation	Option to shut off appliances and compensated
tax this, tax that, tax you, tax the cat, tax everything, tax, tax, tax	tax pollution is ok, some tax is ok
Tax CO2 and do not tax harmful chemicals	Tax harmful pollution - mercury, etc.
Trade carbon credits and tax the people for the carbon	Free to produce energy and sell to anyone
Give data to government, break bill of rights	New markets, new commerce
Struggle with each other	Help each other
Taxation of all value	Free exchange of value
Tyranny Grid	Freedom Grid

7.1 Collectivist Smart Grid: Freedom Smart Grid

Internet and Smart Grid are neutral in this regard

Characteristic	Today's Grid	Smart Grid
Enables active participation by consumers	Consumers are uninformed and non-participative with power system	Informed, involved, and active consumers - demand response and distributed energy resources.
Accommodates all generation and storage options	Dominated by central generation- many obstacles exist for distributed energy resources interconnection	Many distributed energy resources with plug-and-play convenience focus on renewables
Enables new products, services and markets	Limited wholesale markets, not well integrated - limited opportunities for consumers	Mature, well-integrated wholesale markets, growth of new electricity markets for consumers
Provides power quality for the digital economy	Focus on outages - slow response to power quality issues	Power quality is a priority with a variety of quality/price options - rapid resolution of issues
Optimizes assets & operates efficiently	Little integration of operational data with asset management - business process silos	Greatly expanded data acquisition of grid parameters - focus on prevention, minimizing impact to consumers
Anticipates and responds to system disturbances (self-heals)	Responds to prevent further damage- focus is on protecting assets following fault	Automatically detects and responds to problems - focus on prevention, minimizing impact to consumer
Operates resiliently against attack and natural disaster	Vulnerable to malicious acts of terror and natural disasters	Resilient to attack and natural disasters with rapid restoration capabilities

7.2 Smart Grid Characteristics

We take a view that peer to peer technology will spur the generation beyond the smart grid, and not require massive outlays of money. The development will come through millions of individual choices.

Think of a business model similar to the cell phone market. Some big companies put in place the towers, and infrastructure, and the individuals will buy the phones. Can you imagine if you had to buy your cell phone only from an approved vendor and had no choice in the type of phone, price, style, color, and features? This is what is happening now in the smart grid.

The current grid consists of more than 9,000 electric generating units with more than 1,000 gigawatt of generating capacity connected to more than 300,000 miles of transmission lines. Delivery of electricity is a just in time model. As demand is needed, then the product is delivered. Imagine Wal-mart not having any products on the shelves and needing to predict the next days demand each night. Any mistakes in prediction must be fixed with special deliveries or lost in sales. Needing to have the exact amount of energy at all times is expensive and requires a lot of excess capacity. It is very 20th Century.

Industry sets standards for smart grids. Like in computers, banking ATM's wireless networks, the companies can come to common standards to make people able to communicate with each other. The worst possible Smart Grid is one that still uses the old 20th Century hardware – big power plants, power lines and substations – and adds on the 21st Century surveillance systems. Not only does this lead to some sort of scientific overlord scenario but it kills our ability to compete in the world. Even China is moving into a sort of peer to peer energy system – though with some allowance for Big Brother.

Let's compare the Smart Grid as proposed, to a Peer to Peer Electricity model.

Smart Grid	P2P Electric
Informed, involved, and active consumers - demand response and distributed energy resources.	Producers and consumers contact any other producer and consumer
Many distributed energy resources with plug-and-play convenience focus on renewables	Groups can pool their generation and storage into virtual storage and power plants
Mature, well-integrated wholesale markets, growth of new electricity markets for consumers	Third party applications tie in with the grid. Very robust transactions and flexibility.
Power quality is a priority with a variety of quality/price options - rapid resolution of issues	Local micro grids provide more resilience. More backup options in case of faults.
Greatly expanded data acquisition of grid parameters - focus on prevention, minimizing impact to consumers	
Automatically detects and responds to problems - focus on prevention, minimizing impact to consumer	More options to heal restrict access, open to more nodes. Horizontal, and peer sharing.
Resilient to attack and natural disasters with rapid restoration capabilities	More options to go off-grid, local help,

7.3 Smart Grid vs Peer to Peer Electricity

Peer to peer electricity is a natural evolution from the system we have now. The phone system went from centralized AT&T in the 1970's to a very decentralized and inexpensive system around the world.   People can communicate real time through QQ, MSN, and Twitter. The phone systems still need large cables and infrastructure, but most of the innovation has been in decentralized and peer to peer systems on the internet.

Now we add P2P money to the situation - Power Currency.

Smart Grid	P2P Electric	Power Currency
Informed, involved, and active consumers - demand response and distributed energy resources.	Producers and consumers contact any other producer and consumer	Electricity credits can be easily exchanged and used like money. Very portable
Many distributed energy resources with plug-and-play convenience focus on renewables	Groups can pool their generation and storage into virtual storage and power plants	Power Currency easily extends to other commerce, freely trade with food, housing, anything
Mature, well-integrated wholesale markets, growth of new electricity markets for consumers	Third party applications tie in with the grid. Very robust transactions and flexibility.	Huge opportunities for third party software providers to monetize energy
Power quality is a priority with a variety of quality/price options - rapid resolution of issues	Local micro grids provide more resilience. More backup options in case of faults.	Also provides more barter options
Greatly expanded data acquisition of grid parameters - focus on prevention, minimizing impact to consumers		Allows you to transfer electricity into other goods
Automatically detects and responds to problems - focus on prevention, minimizing impact to consumer	More options to heal restrict access, open to more nodes. Horizontal, and peer sharing.	
Resilient to attack and natural disasters with rapid restoration capabilities	More options to go off-grid, local help,	back up options supported by barter systems - switch to fuel, etc.

7.4 Smart Grid: P2P Electric: Power Currency

Some technology advances that will help spur the Smart Grid.

- Buildings that produce much of their own energy.
- Superconducting cables that can carry more energy further.
- Storage for cars, homes, buildings.
- Sensors that make communications and transactions work.

Look at how the internet has evolved. In the 1980's and early 1990's few people could imagine the huge amount of products that the internet would spur. Even five years ago, it would take quite an imagination to come up with that.

Plug in vehicles are the silver bullet. It provides portable power and handles all the major goals of the energy revolution. The Pacific Northwest National Laboratory says that the existing supply of power plants will handle close to 75% of all cars, if they happened to switch to plug in capability and charged overnight. The laboratory claims this would replace 6.2 million barrels of oil per day, or just over half of all imported oil

Scenario - Disaster

The big one hit. 8.2 on the Richter scale. Towers fell, bridges collapsed, it was a nightmare. Hospitals lost their power, transportation was gone, dams fractured. The power grid was out. Blackouts everywhere, which shut off pumps for fuel, fresh water, etc... Waste treatment facilities shut down. Sewage backed up and disease was brewing.

The people were prepared. Thousands of micro grids had been laid - some above ground and some below ground. Cars could run on local bio-diesel, alcohol, ethanol or traditional gasoline.

Most homes had battery systems to save money on peak energy - buy from the grid at night, and use during the day.

Towns had their own portable power plants for much of the same reason.

The biggest thing was the cars ability to run their engines and feed power to the grid. They hooked in the converters which fed power to their homes, neighbors and micro-grids. The micro-grids were up to 50 locations, and could feed to other micro-grids

Many of the micro grids still had problems, but enough were functional that hospitals could get power; pumps could operate and most of the worst effects were prevented. The emergency system kicked in and priorities for power were delivered to make sure that essential services were handled. Of course the owners and operators are compensated for this and compensated well. A small fraction of the cars in the affected area hooked in to the grid and provided more than enough power. The fuels that had to be stored locally such as alcohol, and bio-diesel, were enough to handle one full week, or up to a month with rationing. This was plenty of time to allow relief efforts to arrive and start to get things back to normal. What could have been an aftermath that included disease, deaths, looting, chaos and anarchy, became a situation that was a lot more organized, orderly, peaceful and less severe. This all came about because the millions of people had their own power supplies and fuel. They had this not to prepare for an earthquake, but because it was cheaper to live on and off the grid and to buy and sell in their communities.

FEMA officials came in and tried to round people up and put them into FEMA camps and sports stadiums. With rare situations, there was no need for that.

MOVING POWER PLANTS

Robert Anderson, a Scottish businessman, made the first auto prototype in the 1830s. It ran on batteries. By the end of the 1800's battery powered cars were still outselling gas powered cars and were seen as a toy of the rich. Gas powered cars needed to be cranked to start, and sometimes this was quite dangerous. The electric ignition was a big step to the gas car taking over.

We love to drive our cars. It is part of our culture and reflects our freedom. America has 250 million cars and on average these are driven 12000 miles each year. The developing world is rapidly building auto fleets. In 2010, China became the largest producer and buyer of automobiles. Before 2015, there will be more than twice as many cars sold in China each year, than in the USA.

In the 1990's California and General Motors introduced the EV1, an attempt to mass produce electric vehicles. The venture was such a success that California and General Motors collected all the cars and crushed them.

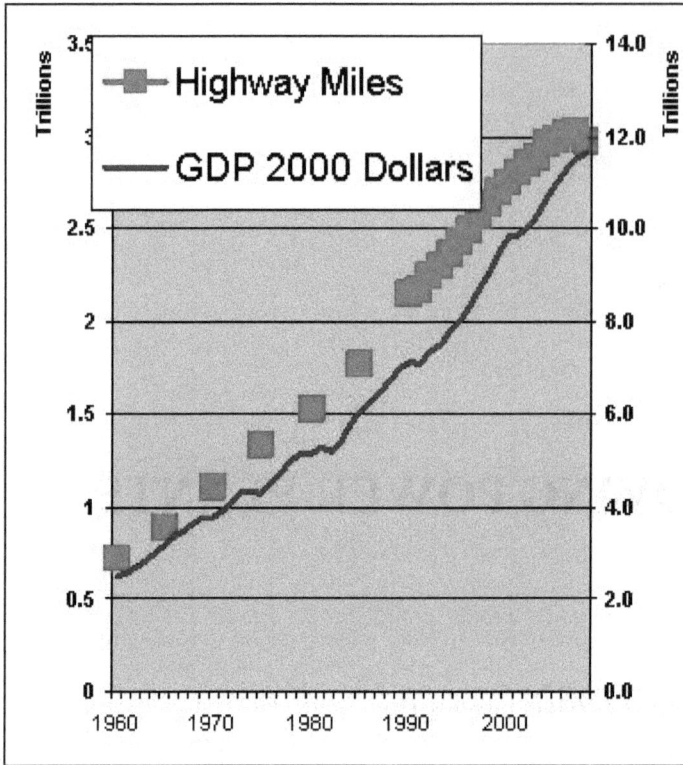

8.1 Highway Miles and GDP

There is a strong relationship between economic growth and using our cars.

We are looking at the very leading edge of the adoption curve. The technology is here that allows electric cars to equal or outperform gas powered cars and the cost of electricity vs. gasoline will get cheaper. Plug in hybrids will be like ipods or mobile phones. There are thousands of scientists in the USA and millions of scientists in Europe and Asia working to find alternatives to gasoline. The solution will probably not come from Texas or Detroit, but from Japan, China or some country that is truly at the mercy of OPEC.

Look at other technology areas - flash memory, hard drives, computer chips, you name it. There will be manufacturing breakthroughs. We will see higher capacity and longer living batteries in BEV and PHEV vehicles.

Not only will electric cars be pollution free, and cost less to operate and maintain, but they will earn income for the owners. Cars will make money for the car owner when the power is needed and the car is parked (such as mid-afternoon) and then retrieve the power when the grid has slack to give, such as on a windy day.

Cost per mile for cars

Gasoline	Electricity
2.50 / gallon	0.10 per KWH
25 miles to gallon	300 watts per mile
10 cents per mile	3 cents per mile

Vehicle to Grid
Vehicle-to-grid (V2G) allows a vehicle to sell power to the grid when it is parked and not in use. When the car batteries need to charge, the flow is reversed and electricity draws from the electrical power grid to charge the battery.

There are about 250 million cars and trucks in the USA. Even abandoned car engines can be used. Most cars are somewhere between 150 and 300 horsepower and heavy duty trucks over 400 HP. For our purposes, we take 200 horsepower as the number. Let's compare the largest power plant in the USA and see how it matches to cars.

Power plant MWH	Power plant Horsepower	Amount of Cars 200 HP/car
1,425	1,910,925	9,554

One KWH = 1.34 horsepower
One MWH = 1340 horsepower

This is theoretical in the year 2010, but who knows in 2020? Networking cars into power plants can work with some inventions. It is theoretical to link ten thousand cars together and expect to get the same output. However, an individual home could use a car for power, especially in a time of emergency such as a hurricane, ice storm, earthquake or war. In that situation, a large power plant may be taken off line or the transmission lines could be brought down.

Until 1994, the US published statistics regarding total horsepower of prime movers. Included in this were power plants, ship engines, farm equipment mines and automobiles. Since then, they do not include autos. Taking recent numbers about power plants and cars on the road and putting an average 200 horsepower per car, we are able to compare the entire electricity industry -nuke, coal, gas, wind, etc. - and compare this to cars.

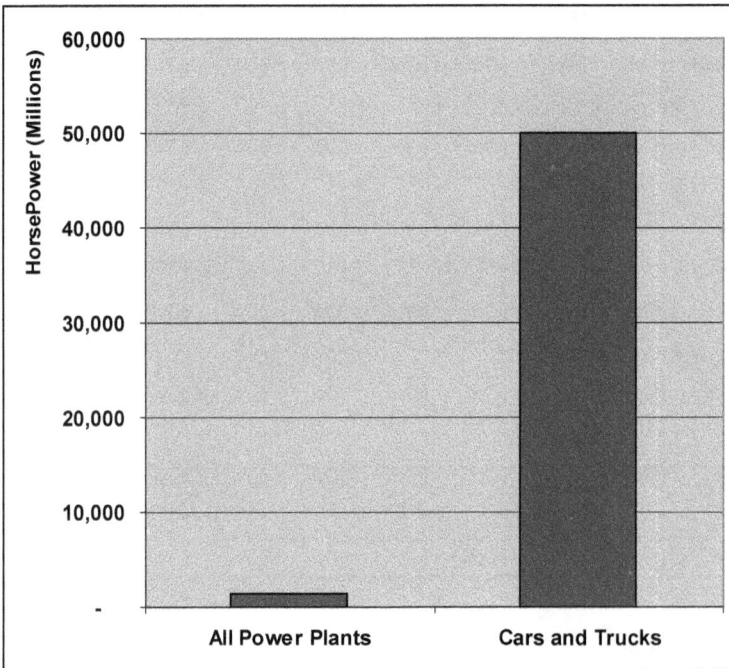

8.2 Horspower: Power Plants and Cars

	All Power Plants in USA	All Cars and Trucks in USA
	17,000	250,000,000
Horsepower	1,504,180,658	50,000,000,000
MWH	1,121,686	37,500,000

Here is the total horsepower of the Auto vs. power plants in 2010

In terms of horsepower, large car companies are the largest power plant producers in the planet. The trick is to tie all these together. If we can tap into this resource, we could increase our energy capacity tenfold. The inventors that can make this happen will be very rich!

These do not need to come from cars in the driveway. Instead of crushing engines, we network them into a system, run as needed, capture pollution, and feed the energy into the grid. We can encase a used car engine and capture exhaust into a filter so there is no noise and air pollution. We could get 1000 old car engines and put them in an array. They turn on and off as needed to power the grid during peak periods, blackouts, etc... We can refit cars with new smaller engines and batteries. The old engines are pulled out and out to use with other power plants.

Utilities require huge fleets of all kinds of vehicles. A dedicated program to push these into BEV and PHEV will be enough to kick start production. The utilities will expand profits and revenue as people move to electric and PHEV. It will be an enormous transfer of wealth from Big Oil, to Big Electric and independent producer. Some utilities like PG&E and PJM are converting their own service fleet to plug in hybrid, and testing out some V2G technology.

There are some other advantages to electric or true hybrid cars in a few years. Cars can be generators. The engine is smaller and simpler. There is flexibility with fuel and power. You can refuel with various sources of electricity or with bio fuels. The hybrid approach opens up a lot of space in the car and gets rid of a lot of the shafts that are needed in conventional vehicles.

	Gas Powered	Hybrid	Electric Worst Now, Can Be Best Later
Cost	Best	Good	
Fuel density	Best	Good	
Fuel cost		Good	Best
Flexibility	Good	Best	
Acceleration	Good		Best
Motor Efficiency		Good	Best
V2G		Good	Best

http://www.eliica.com/English/project/eliica/chassis.html

Hybrid cars coming on the road now can handle 25 miles on all electric. In the US, half the people drive less than 25 miles per day. After the battery runs low, the engine kicks in to drive the car and recharge the batteries. PG&E estimates that though a car battery doesn't have the power to push a car, it still retains a good deal of life (up to 80%) and useable as storage in fixed locations. This helps us to trim off the max load, displaces the need to produce new power plants.

Wind and Cars

Wind is an excellent source of power as it is so cheap now to set up and is approaching the threshold where it will be cheaper than coal. Let's say we put up a large wind farm onshore or offshore. It consists of twenty 2 MWH turbines that produce an average of 150 MWH of electricity per day. However this energy is somewhat unpredictable as the wind is not constant. Now let's combine these with cars. There will always be some cars plugged into the grid. These can take the energy during the off-peak times and feed back during the afternoon peak times. When the wind is blowing the turbines will be feeding straight into the grid. When the wind is not blowing then the grid can suck some juice from the car batteries.

Another great thing about V2G is the ramp up rate or the time it takes to get the electricity onto the grid. Right now, utilities need to keep a large amount of extra capacity on hand. Vehicle to Grid will replace a lot of capital costs. Cars can earn extra money by being the spinning reserves. This opens new financing methods. For example, car owners can finance wind farms. We can have financing schemes offering a car, renewable power capacity, and a guaranteed amount of KWH per week. In an emergency, cars send energy into the grid. Vehicles hook into their local energy grid and provide power to homes, hospitals, etc... Thousands of cars and trucks can feed the grid in these situations and mitigate the effects of a blackout.

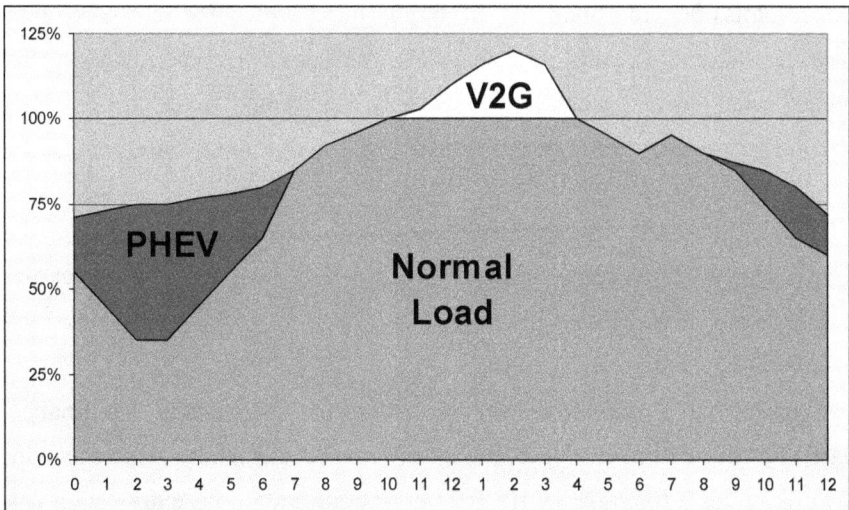

8.3 V2G helps with Peak Load

Scenario - Car Dealer

There are over 20,000 car dealers in the USA.

A rural Car dealer decides to get into the electric business in a big way. He sells all types of cars, and sets up various mechanisms to package energy value with the car.

Later, the Car Manufacturer and Car Dealer Association sets up wind farms financed by a State Bank. This financing supports thousands of consumer loans that include energy production bundled with the cars. Total cost of ownership for the cars and fuel drops 20 percent.

The local dealer has a refurbishing operation. Old cars are stripped of transmission, engine, catalytic converter platinum, and sold off to scrap yards. Some cars get battery packs and small generators and are back on the road.

Car dealer sets up the scheme to sell, finance and wrap financing around car purchases. This is very lucrative for the car dealer as he can make extra commissions on financing of larger purchases. He can earn extra ongoing income streams paid in power currency. He then can use this money many ways – incentives, operation, financing. Later, this develops into fully integrated energy and transportation companies bundling the car and electricity.

The old way: Finance the car over five years at six percent. Owner will pay for gasoline as he uses it.

Alternative way. Finance the car over five years at 6 percent. He finances part of a wind farm at 2 percent interest. The electricity from the wind farm is enough for most of his transportation, and some extra for paying Power Currency into the community.

The 21st Century car is our big advantage.

Truck stop

We don't need to mention the burden 4 or 5 dollar per gallon diesel places on truckers in the USA. The effects multiply throughout the economy. For the small trucker, this energy inflation could put them out of business for good.

Imagine a system in the future that requires little to no diesel, helps solve the energy crisis, prevents electric grid blackouts and brings new sources of wealth to truckers and the trucking industry. Truckers not only have cheap energy, and sell that energy anyone willing to buy it. We have a system where each truck is a mini power plant, and a large truck stop with truckers can have more energy capacity than a coal power plant...

Of course you know the automakers are developing hybrid electric cars, and some of these cars plug in to fill up with energy from the electric grid. There is a perception that only small cars are suitable for this plug-in capability. Is this possible for 18 wheelers? Yes and we look no further than prototypes the US Army and Marines are doing with hybrid trucks and tanks.

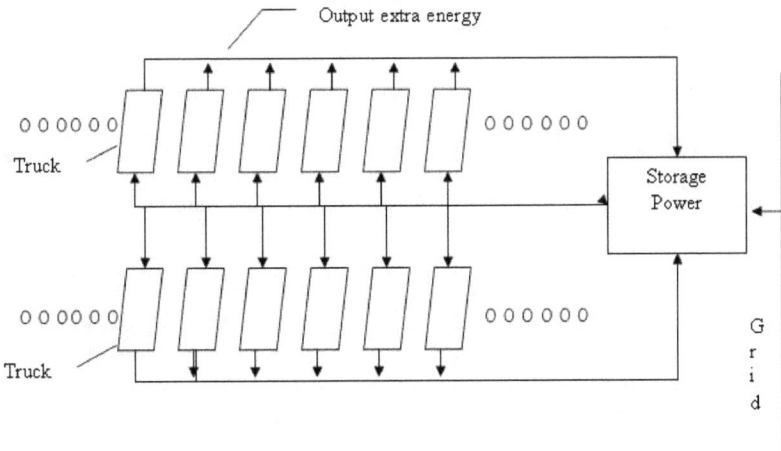

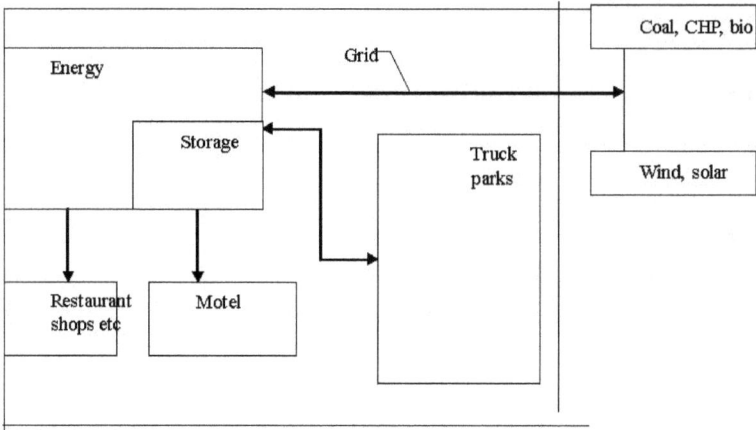

8.4. Truck Stop 2020

PEER TO PEER ELECTRICITY

The networking technology needed for future electricity grids already exists. There is still some work or inventions needed to make the actual low voltage power lines safe and cheap, but the data and accounting systems are far beyond what we need. Banking ATM networks can deliver cash on demand worldwide. Phone apps, instant messaging, MSN, Yahoo Messenger, and such can add new functionality.

Online multi-player games can handle millions of people at a time, all interacting with the game engine and other people. Developing these games and running them requires deep skills in handling complex networks, audits, accounting and technology. The online gaming industry requires large data centers full of hundreds or thousands of computers and networks. The younger generation is very open to new forms of currency. All kinds of game currency (weapons, characters, and digital cash) are traded in virtual currency. They make it, trade it, and use it. Online games like Second Life combine real world money with virtual worlds. People barter among virtual currencies and use real money to buy virtual money.

In China, thousands of gamers work as 'gold farmers', some working more than 12 hour days pounding away online to earn digital money on games like 'World of Warcraft'. This virtual money is sold to people around the world. Tencent is an entertainment portal that targets younger users with online games, instant messaging, and e-commerce services. They use a 'Q coin' to allow people to upgrade their online status, buy virtual tools for games, share music, etc... People buy one Q coin with one RMB (15 US cents). A few years ago, people could buy real world items with Q Coins, and then China's Central Bank stepped in to put limits and regulations on the virtual currency. Tencent, also developed a platform called Tenpay, that gives corporate and individuals a means to transact online with real money. The company acts as a clearing platform with a range of value added services. They work with the top banks in China to facilitate the transactions, and earn micropayments on the transactions.[x] Tencent claims to have more than 200 million people using virtual money. The government is looking to tax virtual money at a rate of 3 percent on each transaction[xi].

We talked earlier about exponential growth as a way that paper money gets debased and destroyed. We have all seen the consistent growth in technology in computers, phones, and televisions. We see this exponential growth can work in systems like Facebook, Google, and Twitter to grow lightning fast. These jumps can come from a number of areas

Technology   Marketing   Inventions   Art
Celebrity Endorsements   New Selling Systems
Distribution Systems   Social causes   Willpower.

The power of exponential growth has spurred rapid advances in technology. The adoption of a new currency system is very rapid if people can earn benefits by forming groups. Remember the MCI friends and family program?

Take a calendar. If you put one dollar on January 1, then double to two on

January 2, four on the 3rd, eight on the 4th and so on. You will start running into real money in the second and third week. At the end of the month, you will have over one billion dollars. Facebook grew like this over a period of just a few years. Power Currency can do the same – especially if it is legal.

Here are some simple scenarios for exponential growth with Power Currency backed by clean energy.

- One person recruits another to join (2)
- One person increases their own capacity every six months
- Two people recruit more
- Social networking sites set up
- Invite investment into renewable energy
- Social networks expand
- adding more demands on the system
- putting in more engines
- these machines will also feed more engines

Energy production continues to grow. There is a limit, but this limit is not reached for quite a while. And by the time we get there, we will discover more sources of energy in outer space.

Rapid growth in energy is happening around the world, though at a State level. Over the next five years, China will add the same amount of electricity power generation, as the United States has already installed in its entire history up to 2009. They do this through large coal plants, nuclear reactors, and wind farms.

So let's see what it would take to double our installed capacity. In 2009 we had 1,000 GWH of generating power. Most of this was produced in central power plants powered by nuke, gas and coal. This could be doubled if each home had 10 KW of capacity or each car had 5 KW of capacity. This is not difficult to happen with some innovation. In 1980, only a few people (Bill Gates was one of them) thought that every home could have a computer.

Once solar gets cheap, batteries get cheap or there is a breakthrough with cars, then this will happen. We will not need to build anymore large nuke or solar plants.

A large retailer like Sears, Walmart or Home Depot can drive the business. Any US State could implement programs that would make a tipping point. States that push forward early would be the rich states. They get the jobs, royalties and the accrued wealth. It would show other states, and then off we go.

If there are technical or social breakthroughs in solar and wind energy, they will crowd oil, gas and coal out of the mix. Digital cameras used to be very expensive. Once a tipping point hit, then they took 99 percent of the market from cameras that require film and processing. We will see the same when there is a breakthrough in solar energy. Fuel for solar and wind is free. Digital photos are free; film photos cost money to buy and process. Solar fuel is free; oil and gas cost money to get, distribute and use.

With the power of such high growth, the biggest deterrent is government involvement and special interests. The best thing the Government can do is to allow the entrepreneurial spirit to flourish. The second best thing governments can do is to provide incentives and tax breaks. Even tax the bad fuel to spur on the good.

Decentralized energy let's us take a new look at this energy situation. Let's start at the grass roots and work your way up to the national level, going from individuals, through groups, neighborhoods, companies, towns, on up to national level.

There is a case to be said for grassroots level power generation. The power of a small number compounded many times, is very strong. Any person, company, city or state can take the lead. Once the first one is successful, then others will follow. The early adopters will get a small short term financial return on their own investment but an additional emotional return on investment. They will get a jump on what will become a great new market.

In the future we will see millions of cars with energy, along with millions of small energy units at fixed locations. This offers a great opportunity for them to trade directly with each other. Peer-to-peer (P2P) is a collaboration model that ties together computing resources to link straight with each other over a network. Most people associate P2P with file sharing and the negative connotations of illegal downloading of movies. Once Peer to Peer Electricity takes off, then the economic benefits will wipe out resistance. If the US Federal Government kills this, then it will take hold in other countries, and come back to America ten or twenty years later.

Some additional benefits that will help drive networking and group development.

Added land value. We have an abundance of land to produce electricity and bio fuels. Much of the land useless for farming or grazing is suitable for solar or wind energy. The land is available for less than 1000 USD per acre. Putting energy on this land will increase the income ability of the land and drive up the land values, not to mention the land owner's balance sheet. Farms use land for biofuel plants, processing, etc...

Avoided capacity Costs and New financing opportunities. Many states have a standard contract for small power producers when they negotiate with the big utilities. A group of 500 New Yorkers could pool resources and set up a 500 MW wind farm. They get paid in kwcash and sell excess to others. Some will donate to charity; some will sell, etc...

Many small beat few large. Large power plants can take many years to build - nuclear power plants over ten years, large coal plants perhaps five years. Small distributed energy systems can be built and working in weeks, days or even hours. Some successful entrepreneurs will become gigawattaires.

Any one of the following sectors could do enough to push this over the edge. Any one of these can make the difference. They can use the revenue models we will cover in the next chapter.

Corporations use scale to set up large systems. Employees, and even customers or suppliers can buy into the plants and share in the output. Companies like Google, Apple, Home Depot, and Walmart can make the whole thing happen.

Associations have a great opportunity to drive new energy. They can pool their member's resources and build large scale systems. Then the members will enjoy the resulting credits which they can use, trade, purchase, and sell. One association like the National Automobile Dealer Association can make a huge difference. The NADA would provide the framework for their 20000 member car dealers to join. Then these dealers pass membership benefits onto their customers.

Universities are an excellent source of early adopters. They can subsidize these activities. They can build new vehicles, new energy and so on. They also sit on a lot of land and can install the energy devices. Vehicles on campus tend to travel locally and easily move to all electric or PHEV.

Research Institutions, like universities, are sitting on large amounts of land and have the resources to build things for the long term without requiring immediate ROI.

Industry Groups. Companies within certain industry groups will come together and collaborate on these solutions. For example the high tech industry could push for their supply chains and customers to get onto renewable energy. Software and hardware companies will form together and do this. IT companies could establish pricing models where they are paid in energy. IBM, Cisco, Microsoft, Intel, Oracle, all could earn huge profits in terms of Power Currency.

Financial Institutions. Banks that have bad loans can use this to fix their balance sheets. They cannot sell the bad asset but they put some renewable energy sources on distressed properties and sell the energy.

Utilities are an obvious candidate for early adopter as they have the infrastructure in place. Many states are mandating that the utilities will have a certain percent renewable by a certain date. They have the customer base.

Eco-Activists are important. They pay a higher price to be on the leading edge. People who buy the new Tesla pay three times the price of a normal car.

Manufacturers have some good assets that be reenergized. Many also have power plants that can work on weekends.

Stock Exchanges have the trading platform in place to bring this to market. They can pull in members to buy into the renewable energy.

States. States have the resources, land, and people. A state could wipe out its own debt and add funds to pensions with energy.

Military. The logistics requirements of fuel are difficult in remote locations. Vehicles on the battlefield will provide the power for new laser weapon systems.

Now, within anyone of these sectors, or from the ground up, let's go into how these can tie together and communicate. Let's look at this from simple to complex.

Most basic level. At this level, it is just the customer and another customer, or the utility. The customer may have an electric vehicle, own power supply, or live entirely off the grid. They may deploy some batteries to buy cheap energy at night and go off grid during the peak expensive periods.

9.1 P2P two homes

At the most basic level two nodes representing end users can communicate and conduct a transaction. They would exchange at least two messages related to negotiation of an energy supply from one to the other. With this transaction, energy can flow from one to the other. The messages will be in a standard format such as EDI, XML or some future language.

Local level. In a group of homes on a street, or small neighborhood, the participants will buy and sell from each other. When there is a shortage, some local resources can kick in, such as a car or generator. The transactions stay local. It can tap into the small energy sources at customer's homes and vehicles. The local transformer will distributed power within its network, and the transactions are accounted locally.

This will open up new capacity for electric automobiles to recharge while absorbing potential strain on the power grid. Electric energy companies will achieve better efficiencies. They will save investment costs on existing poles, wires, stations and plants. They will have more new sources of high profit revenue as they broker energy transactions. This will help to relieve power grid bottlenecks and constraints.

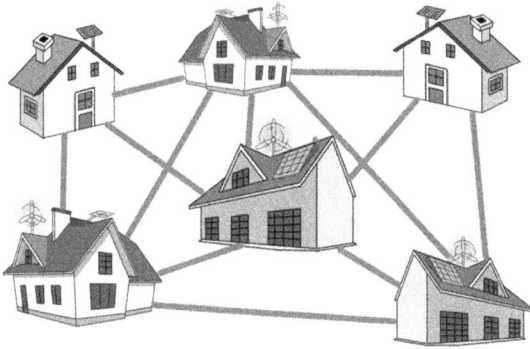

9.2 P2P street

Town level. This has robust protection, communications, networking, and safety systems. Here is where communities start to develop sophisticated solutions. We start to see virtual power plants. If you take a large number of small systems and make them appear and act as one larger power plant then you have a virtual power plant. In this environment, all the pieces are virtualized and combined to look like one larger resource.

Each virtual environment is managed and developed from scratch. There are many environments, from a small two node system, to something that takes place nationwide. It can be industry groups, affiliations, sports teams' promotions, coffee shops, chain stores, and peer to peer networks, any-thing...

County, State Level. Here we see larger networks and Virtual Power Plants. Whole robust communities will evolve. Each location can have a number of power generating devices, and each of those have a unique identification. For example, a small business has a solar array, wind turbine, battery packs and some vehicles with batteries. There can also be many nodes in remote areas such as a wind farm or solar concentrator. Then as two or more join they can have one time or long term relationships and transactions. Once the other sources are identified then the users swap or transact energy.

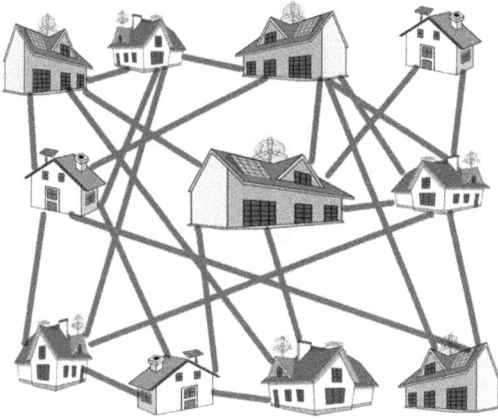

9.3 P2P neighborhood

People within a P2P network create connections with others forming a group of two or more.   Applications are endless. Group systems set up where people opt into a virtual network of energy users and savers that use a series of business rules to swap or trade energy back and forth.

We have seen Peer-to-peer networks expand very quickly. Technology will drive breakthroughs that make local power generation cheaper and more convenient.   What is new is the emerging trend for individuals to become power producers and owners of the means to produce, then to share these resources with others. The benefits reach across many owners and make the overall system much more valuable. A network of ten users will make a virtual power plant that gives back twenty times the benefit.

Peer to peer is not new. There were earlier sorts of applications that used this type of system. SABRE travel reservations started in the 1960's and used a lot of P2P concepts. Car dealers have had peer to peer commerce systems for decades. They are able to locate parts and order directly from other car dealers. Car Dealer A could send out a parts request to a local network of dealers and quickly get an answer of availability, price and delivery time. This was first put into work in the 80's and was standard practice for car dealers in the USA in the 1990's. The communications to make this happen went through a central hub, and though expensive by today's standards, it worked very well and was big business.

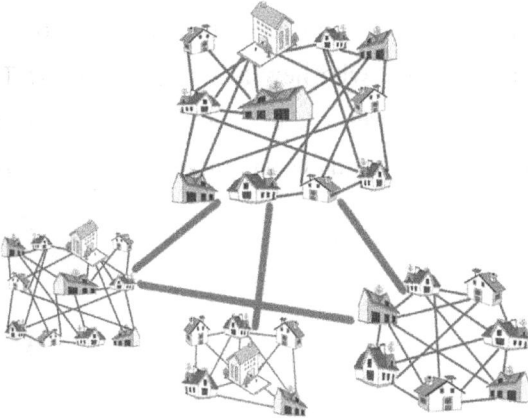

9.4 P2P Town and Up

Without this, the parts departments would rely on phone calls and higher inventory amounts. The vendor provided a valuable service to make this work and was rewarded very well.

The direct buying and selling of power will also free up space on the traditional large transmission lines, as buyers and sellers can deliver over local power networks. A lot of these networks will need to be set up from scratch, but that is part of the whole economic growth model.

Energy distribution will be more dispersed and rely less on large power plants at the ends of the energy supply chain. The slack in the end of the power grid can absorb enormous additional capacity that could not occur in a top down centralized approach as we now have. This will be especially useful in blackouts, ice storms, and disaster situations. A distributed grid resists a military attack against the power grid. It would be much harder to take down the entire grid if the bottlenecks have multiple workarounds and backups. It can help to isolate problems and thus provide fault containment that would not be possible otherwise.

There will be many applications that tie into other forms of entertainment and parts of our lives. Think what sports can do to leverage their brands into fabulous multiplayer games. Also, with new technology like 3D TV, holograms home entertainment complexes, the electricity required will be huge. This grows the use of electricity, builds wealth and creates jobs.

KW CASH

A major franchise retail store decides to promote clean energy as part of its corporate social responsibility. They offer clean KWH credits to their customers.

These credits are used as cash. The customers use this as gifts or make purchases at other locations. The store opens a membership club. A percentage of sales from customers go into a membership pool for renewable energy. The store keeps half and the customers get credit for their proportion. The more they purchase, the more they get credits.

This nationwide retail store sets up a remote site for low cost concentrated solar power of more than 100 MW installed capacity and some wind energy shares. Each store installs PV cells, small wind and battery banks.

Excess power is sold to customers who have PHEV and come to the store to shop. They are given free KWH if they buy more than 50 dollars in any one trip. If the stores, cannot fulfill their energy requirements then they buy from the grid at prevailing rates. At nighttime they load up on cheap base load energy, and use that during the day.

Power Currency is designed to work within the existing financial and energy systems. There are unlimited revenue and pricing models. Secure, trusted tools manage the relationships between consumers, suppliers, and service providers. All kinds of plans can be put together. Transactions tie in with the energy management systems.

A wide range of service providers participate. Agents and third parties produce, distribute and provide information or transaction services. These provide customers with access to range of suppliers and producers from multiple sources. They use some means to identify and group customers according to class, location, etc... An agent's business model will let it add a premium as they are bringing economies of scale and provided services to the marketplace. They add efficiencies, guarantees, financing, and pull together groups to bring in discounts.

Service providers will be a very important part of the growth of this process. Service providers provide excellent services in the paper money system we have now, and can use many of the same tools and talents to build the Power Currency economy. They open many new business models, push viral marketing and build the exponential growth. In addition to the financial aspects, there are all kinds of data applications here. These are tied in with marketing, vehicle use, media, telecom, and endless other applications. Marketing related information tied to demographic, income, and other factors are used. These can add new levels of opportunities for incentives, and discounts. These also bring about schemes for bundling. For example, an air conditioner is sold with a set amount of kilowatts that are financed. Groups of individuals can come together in a peer to peer method to form a buying group.

There are great opportunities for software companies, consulting companies and any sort of service provider. They not only will figure out great ways to bring these to the market but they will be able to have an extra layer that gets transaction revenue. This will provide long term steady income

Let's look at a few business models from least to greater complexity.

The first scenario is a simple one – a direct transaction where a customer has a direct link to the source of energy. They will use a clearinghouse to manage the transaction. The clearinghouse is tied in with the utility.

Revenue Pricing Model One

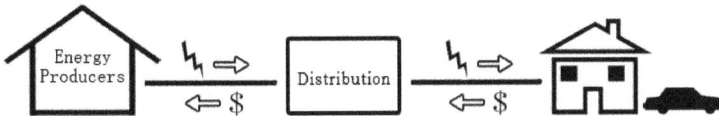

10.1 KW Cash two homes

This simple model shows electricity and money each going in one direction. Here the energy producer gets 77 percent of the revenue, and the various other participants get 23 percent.

Energy Producer	77%
Utility	10%
3rd Part	5%
Info Tech Provider	5%
Local Tax	2%
Tax	1%

These splits shown here are arbitrary and chang however the parties wish. Then in terms of raw KWH numbers we split things out below.

Participants	50 KWH	Service Providers	Tax	
Energy Producer	38.5	2.5	1	
Utility	5			
3rd Part	2.5		0.5	
Total	46	2.5	1.5	50

The various business rules added (e.g. pricing, time, importance criteria, min/max, and limits) by the energy supplier, energy management system and the users will let all parties to optimize and negotiate benefits to both sides. The third parties make a small amount in each transaction but will make huge amounts across the millions of transactions they do. Right now gaming companies make a fraction of a penny for each transaction, but make millions of dollars in profit per years.

Revenue Pricing Model Two

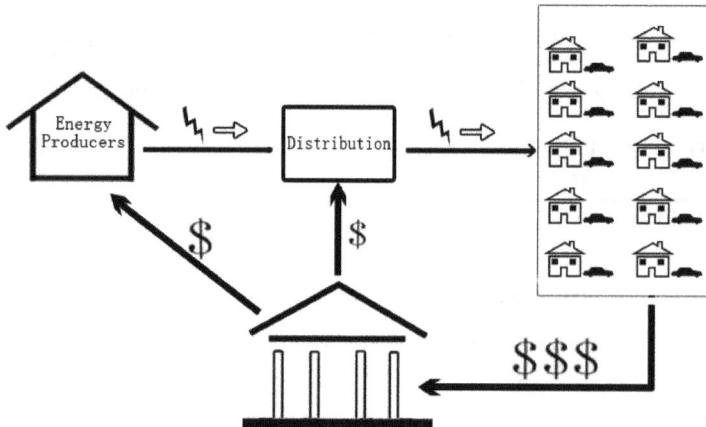

10.2 KW Cash Neighborhood

Now let's take it further and add in a whole range of agents. These can be appliance manufacturers, stores, coffee shops, car dealers and on and on. Maybe they subscribe to an organization such as a credit card company, or non-profit organization. The agent will claim a portion as markup.

We start with a similar share as before, but there are more parties to take taxes or fees for services.

Energy Producer	77%
Utility	10%
3rd Party	5%
Info Tech Provider	3%
Agent	2%
Local Tax	2%
National Tax	1%

So as we convert these percentages out among the players, we come up with the following Power Currency.

Participants	80 KWH	Service Providers		Tax		
Energy Producer	61.6	Info Tech	2.4	1.6		
Utility	8	Agent	1.6			
3rd Party	4			0.8		
Total	73.6		4	2.4	80	

The transactions are as simple or as complex as the parties want. Home-owners, business owners, and service providers set up their own preferences. All the communications and programming are set up by computer companies, utilities and others. A financial clearinghouse comes in to make sure that all participants are compensated.

This level of commerce would not take too much time to establish. Within a few years, we can see this in operation. Vehicle to grid operations, small towns, remote communities, and all sorts of other scenarios can use this simple model. As mentioned earlier, all kinds of third parties can get involved and drive these revenue models. In fact, it makes sense for some IT entrepreneurs to set up these simple systems. They will be able to tap into two of the biggest industries we have – energy and finance.

Applications are endless. Long-term regulated agreements are put in place to provide incentives to buy electric powered cars and renewable energy. The business rules can also apply to the communications and screen for other like-minded participants.   Let's look at a model which has more emphasis on third party agents.

Revenue Pricing Model Three

This figure shows how numerous agents may be included in a transaction. The payment is split among an energy producer, utility, agent, 4th parties and multiple sources at some of these levels.

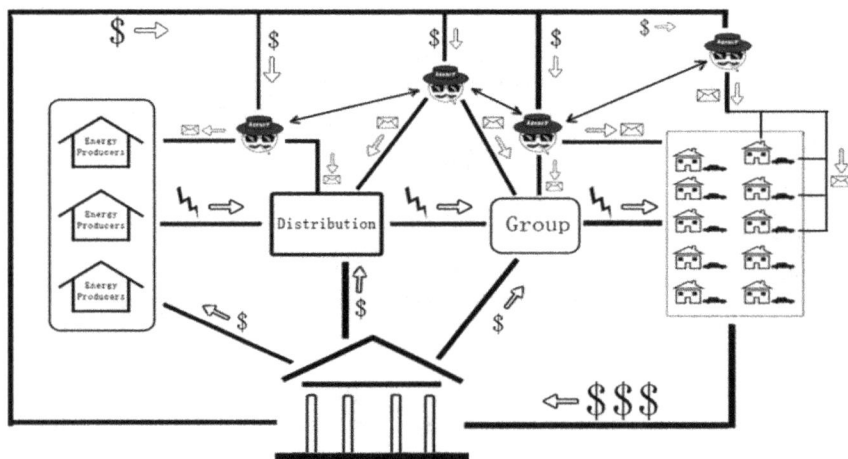

10.3 KW Cash Economy

The Agent contacts get a request to fill an energy need and contacts the customer. They have a previous agreement in place that could cover any range of parameters, like selling during peak demand and buying during dips. So the communication between them goes back and forth - contact, negotiate and confirm. Many times this will be computers and machines talking to other computers and machines based on established agreements already in place.

The data is valuable and used in developing new efficiencies in the market. The clearinghouses that collect this data can analyze and provide to others for income or efficiencies. The table shows how a data clearinghouse can profit from handling and processing data.

Energy Producer	77%
Utility	10%
3rd Party	5%
Info Tech Provider	2%
Agent	1%
Financial company	1%
Data Company	1%
Local Tax	2%
National Tax	1%

Membership in groups comes into play now and adds to viral marketing and the spread of Power Currency transactions. Membership could have discounts for classes like retirees or veterans or alumni, political affiliation, common ideals, religion, sports teams, newspaper subscribers.

Membership Cards protects the proper use of discounts, improves distribution efficiency, and improves the customer's ease-of-use. Agents and vendors that use these pay an additional service charge or receive payment as determined in the business rules.

130KWH		Service Providers	Tax		
Participants					
Energy Producer	100.1	I.T.	2.6	2.6	
Utility	13	Agent	1.3		
3rd Party		Financial company			
	6.5	pany	1.3	1.3	
		Data Company	1.3		
Total	119.6		6.5	3.9	130

This will lead to great incentives for energy production, and promotion among users. There are two main processes here (1) the information sharing and negotiation and (2) the financial transaction This level can hand off the data and transaction to a third party that provides clearing services for the transaction. This third party can be the utility or a software company.

Energy Producer	77%
Utility	10%
3rd Party	5%
Info Tech Provider	1%
Agent	0.5%
Financial company	1%
Data Company	1%
Member/Clubs	1%
Services Companies	0.5%
Local Tax	2%
National Tax	1%

After the contract there are reporting structures in place on service performance, variances and delivery. The transactions are automated by rules and artificial intelligence.

	200 KWH	Service Providers		Tax	
Energy Producer Utility	154	Info Tech	2	4	
3rd Par-ty	20	Agent Financial	1		
	10	company	2	2	
		Data Company	2		
		Member/Clubs	2		
		Services Co.	1		
Total	184		10	6	200

The various business rules added (e.g. pricing, time, importance criteria, min/max, and limits) by the energy supplier, energy management system and the users will let all parties optimize and negotiate benefits to both sides. This provides new areas of optimization at the user level, group level or across the entire grid. This allows mass personalization of decisions and also at the higher level for inventory of energy to be gathered and optimized across a wide area.

Superdistribution

We have seen companies like Google, Facebook and Groupon explode in popularity.

Superdistribution models let customers become redistributors. This ties in very well with the grouping method and recruiting drives that can spur renewable energy. Customers can become group leaders and earn overrides on transactions. They can also develop multi-level models of sales and distribution. The following shows how this might work.

Superdistribution concept has been around for 20 years. Japanese professor Ryoichi Mori at the Institute of Information Sciences and Electronics looked proposed that people could forward electronic content to others so they could try before they buy. Then they would have a mechanism in place to get paid automatically and securely. The interests of all the participants are protected. No firm agreement is needed and the change of money is automatic for all parties.

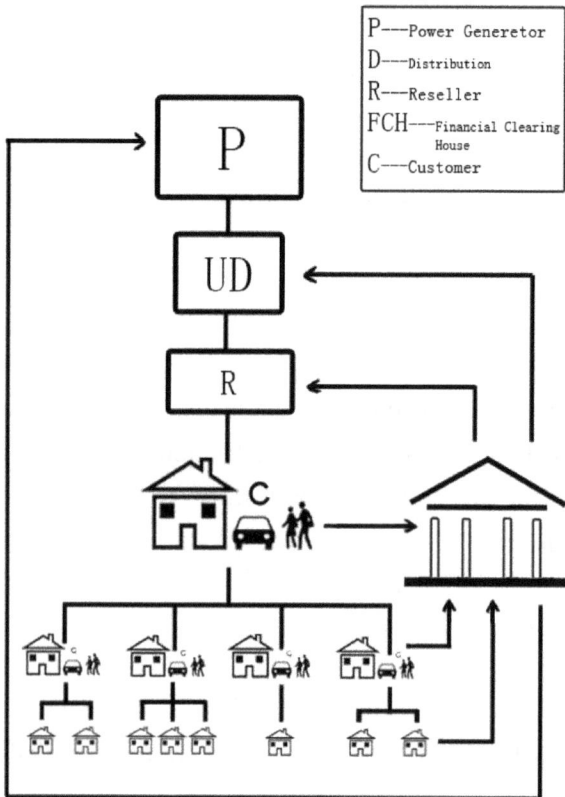

P---Power Generetor
D---Distribution
R---Reseller
FCH---Financial Clearing House
C---Customer

10.4. Superdistribution

As applied here, the electric content is the information and financial transactions. The electricity is sent and delivered through the electric grid or newer smart micro-grids. The information and transactions are matched with the actual delivery through computer programming and accounting systems.

Let's dream of a scenario where this can happen with Power Currency. An unleashed distributed power network could see enormous growth in energy. With an annual growth rate that is very moderate by internet standards, we could see:

- double installed electricity capacity by 2020 and double again by 2030.
- cut pollution 50 to 90 percent from present levels
- cut out all oil imports to a negligible level and start to export energy again.

JAMES ROGERS

STATE AND LOCAL SOLUTIONS

"The privilege of creating and issuing money is not only the supreme prerogative of government, but it is the government's greatest creative opportunity."

Abraham Lincoln

We are seeing stress within the states – asset sales, loss of jobs, cuts in services, destruction of pensions, and misery. Most States have budget deficits and then feel compelled to sell real assets to pay off credit money debt that was created out of thin air.

During the Great Depression, thousands of cities issued local scrip. Now many states like California face a terrible budget deficit. One proposal is to issue IOUs to their State workers. The IOUs or scrip are not forced on vendors but they are used as money for any State tax or service. This is enough to provide a market for the scrip. The IOUs are redeemable at some time in the future though with some added interest attached.

So a vendor could receive these IOUs instead of Federal Reserve Notes and use the IOU for state college tuition or taxes. Because the State accepted the warrants, the IOUs have value and are accepted among the citizens.

The Constitution states.

Article I, Section. 10. No State shall enter into any Treaty, Alliance, or Confederation; grant Letters of Marque and Reprisal; coin Money; emit Bills of Credit; make any Thing but gold and silver Coin a Tender in Payment of Debts; pass any Bill of Attainder, ex post facto Law, or Law impairing the Obligation of Contracts, or grant any Title of Nobility.

Paper IOUs are workable for emergencies, but go against the restrictions in the Constitution. Power Currency provides a stronger solution and keeps the politicians from printing too many paper IOUs. Setting up a system to issue money, the State will never have a deficit (unless they want), can wipe out unnecessary interest payments and expand its economy. One way to issue legal money is with coins that mix in a small portion of a grain of silver or gold. The coins can be in KWH or MWH denominations. The coins would not have enough gold or silver to attract financial elements that will gather them up and take them out of circulation. It would be closer to the spirit of the Constitution than Federal Reserve Notes.

A local based currency backed by energy with a national currency for trade will work well together. Currency that is restricted geographically tied in with the local electricity grid will be even stronger. If a State is producing 50 gigawatts of electricity per day, then they could issue 5 gigawatts worth of coins for circulation. In theory, the person could submit coins for payment of their energy bill or pay taxes, and the State can use the coins to pay energy bills.

Many British Commonwealth countries have two or more currencies. The Isle of Guernsey in the British Channel issued a limited amount of money into circulation and was able to build infrastructure, buildings and other projects. These Guernsey pounds are spent into existence for public works, and are taken out of circulation to pay for fees and taxes.

During the currency crisis in Argentina in 2000, some provinces issued their own money which returned as taxes. The population accepted this. This was short lived but helped through some rough months. The national government swapped them out with pesos in 2003.

So having a parallel currency could work. Here are some steps.

1. Issue interest bearing IOUs to State workers, contractors and to people who receive tax refunds. These are used in the future for payment of taxes and have a redemption date before which they cannot be cashed. Something like issued: 2011, redeemable: 2014 − 2015.

2. Assert this as real local money. As this is accepted within the community, more people will use the money. Local retailers, restaurants, and merchants will accept the money so it becomes widespread.

3. Eventually, you will have two (or more) currencies - regional money, national/international money.

Local money works best as it fosters cooperation among the community. The money stays local. Federal Reserve Notes are debt based money that drains from the local community out to large money centers and foreign countries. All money is issued as debt. Since the debt needs to be paid back, there is a limit to growth, and there is a shift from the productive forces in society to the money changers.

Each state will have its own priority and solution
    Hawaii – Displace oil, waves
    KY – Coal, biomass
    Arizona – Solar
    PA – natural gas,
    offshore wind with DE

An approach is to consider Public Trusts and Public Credit. State resources such as minerals, land, ports and such are used to back local money. The backing is handled through a State Bank. States should never sell off such assets, but can use them for the common good and as the foundation for local money.

Public Infrastructure and public works projects work well. Some of the public works programs in the 1930s were very effective. The Hoover Dam, Tennessee Valley Authority and thousands of other projects put people to work and spent money into the economy. Get debt free money into the economy through business loans to build public sector projects, agricultural support, salaries and welfare payments.

You can build large networks of renewable energy systems. This is strong in an economy that has a lot of productive talent. Convert old factories to new factories. As this is distributed around the community, it will be enough to stimulate the new economy. Without the usury that explodes the debt, a local money system can grow much faster than the usury Federal Reserve System. Without usury overhanging all production, the prices of items will be cut in half and quite competitive with 'Made in China'. In fact, production in China is financed at zero percent and in a lot of cases is subsidized at about fifteen percent.

By now, you know that I like to use tables and graphs to make a point. Lets look at the asssets of States. First, the United States.

State		UNITED STATES
Power generation	Megawatts	1,121,686
Population		307,006,550
Total land	Square Miles	3,537,438
Housing Units		129,969,653
Farm land	Acres	922,095,840
Cars (est.)		227,446,893

11.1 Some USA Stats

Every State has an abundance of resources. Land, people, cars, homes. These can all be put to use in a free market way.

Imagine a road going from A to B. Now there are different ways to block this road such as a small ditch, a wall, and a river with no bridge. The individual can fill in the ditch but getting his own power supply and helping his neighbors. The entrepreneur can become a billionaire, or gigawattaire, by find a way around the wall. He can invent a networking tool that ties cars and homes together. The State can build the bridge by passing laws, cutting down regulation, opening up lands, and setting up financing options for people to use.

Each State has the resources right now to make this happen. Here is a listing of the resources from the Census and EIA

State	Power (MWH) MWH	Population	Farmland (acres) Acres	Homes	Cars (est.)
ALABAMA	34,021	4,708,708	9,033,537	2,182,343	3,819,100
ALASKA	2,212	698,473	881,585	283,878	496,787
ARIZONA	29,548	6,595,778	26,117,899	2,752,991	4,817,734
ARKANSAS	16,474	2,889,450	13,872,862	1,310,624	2,293,592
CALIFORNIA	70,933	36,961,664	25,364,695	13,433,718	23,509,007
COLORADO	14,744	5,024,748	31,604,911	2,167,850	3,793,738
CONNECTICUT	8,714	3,518,288	405,616	1,445,825	2,530,194
DELAWARE	3,511	885,122	510,253	396,222	693,389
FLORIDA	67,343	18,537,969	9,231,570	8,852,754	15,492,320
GEORGIA	39,639	9,829,211	10,150,539	4,063,548	7,111,209
HAWAII	2,805	1,295,178	1,121,329	515,625	902,344
IDAHO	3,785	1,545,801	11,497,383	647,502	1,133,129
ILLINOIS	50,053	12,910,409	26,775,100	5,292,016	9,261,028
INDIANA	30,990	6,423,113	14,773,184	2,809,559	4,916,728
IOWA	15,809	3,007,856	30,747,550	1,344,080	2,352,140
KANSAS	13,576	2,818,747	46,345,827	1,234,057	2,159,600
KENTUCKY	23,970	4,314,113	13,993,121	1,934,973	3,386,203
LOUISIANA	30,116	4,492,076	8,109,975	1,963,354	3,435,870
MAINE	4,658	1,318,301	1,347,566	704,578	1,233,012
MARYLAND	13,550	5,699,478	2,051,756	2,341,194	4,097,090
MASS.	15,358	6,593,587	517,879	2,748,321	4,809,562
MICHIGAN	33,080	9,969,727	10,031,807	4,541,680	7,947,940

State				
MINNESOTA	16,259	5,266,214	26,917,962	2,332,916	4,082,603
MISSISSIPPI	17,769	2,951,996	11,456,241	1,282,090	2,243,658
MISSOURI	22,460	5,987,580	29,026,573	2,682,066	4,693,616
MONTANA	5,904	974,989	61,388,462	441,279	772,238
NEBRASKA	8,247	1,796,619	45,480,358	791,863	1,385,760
NEVADA	13,160	2,643,085	5,865,392	1,137,997	1,991,495
N. HAMPSHIRE	4,513	1,324,575	471,911	600,090	1,050,158
NEW JERSEY	20,082	8,707,739	733,450	3,526,453	6,171,293
NEW MEXICO	8,893	2,009,671	43,238,049	878,043	1,536,575
NEW YORK	43,104	19,541,453	7,174,743	8,017,881	14,031,292
N. CAROLINA	30,103	9,380,884	8,474,671	4,258,625	7,452,594
N. DAKOTA	6,297	646,844	39,674,586	316,435	553,761
OHIO	36,462	11,542,645	13,956,563	5,094,126	8,914,721
OKLAHOMA	22,892	3,687,050	35,087,269	1,650,387	2,888,177
OREGON	14,524	3,825,657	16,399,647	1,639,498	2,869,122
PENNSYLVANIA	49,787	12,604,767	7,809,244	5,518,558	9,657,477
RHODE ISLAND	2,020	1,053,209	67,819	452,191	791,334
S. CAROLINA	25,790	4,561,242	4,889,339	2,084,231	3,647,404
S. DAKOTA	3,500	812,383	43,666,403	365,563	639,735
TENNESSEE	23,207	6,296,254	10,969,798	2,780,857	4,866,500
TEXAS	111,848	24,782,302	130,398,753	9,724,220	17,017,385
UTAH	7,803	2,784,572	11,094,700	952,999	1,667,748
VERMONT	1,108	621,760	1,233,313	314,246	549,931
VIRGINIA	25,833	7,882,590	8,103,925	3,330,465	5,828,314
WASHINGTON	30,629	6,664,195	14,972,789	2,814,238	4,924,917
W. VIRGINIA	17,250	1,819,777	3,697,606	893,771	1,564,099
WISCONSIN	18,559	5,654,774	15,190,804	2,587,350	4,527,863
WYOMING	7,948	544,270	30,169,526	249,388	436,429

11.2 State Resources

So pick your state. So each State has the resources it needs to develop wealth. Land, people, buildings, homes, businesses, cars, farmlands. It's all there to build upon.

Let's pick Maryland.

13 GWH (13 million KWH) of power plant capacity. A good start.

People: 5.7 million people. Lots of entrepreneurs and financing opportunities.

Farmland: Two million acres. A few percent of this could grow bio fuels. The waste and residue from farms, can be converted to bio-fuels.

Homes: Two million homes. On average if each home had the capacity to make 10 KW of energy, and store 2 KW of energy, then we will have 20 million KW of production (20 GWH) and 4 million KW of storage

Cars: Four million cars. Let's say five percent of those can network and produce energy daily, and 25 percent can plug in during blackouts or emergencies. Each car can on average deliver 20 KWH. Then we have a further 4 million KWH (4 GWH) daily and 20 million KWH (20 GWH) during emergencies.

Now, the Constitution restricts states from issuing its own money unless it is in gold and silver. Let's design some coins to represent the money. For now we will call these Bolts and Zaps. A Bolt is 1 MWH and a Zap is 10 KWH.

	Zaps	Gold	Silver	Energy
		grains	grains	KWH
Bolt	100.00	1		1000
½ Bolt	50.00	.5		500
¼ Bolt	25.00	.25		250
Zap	1.00		1	10
½ Zap	0.50		.5	5
¼ Zap	0.25		.25	2.5
.1 Zap	0.10		.1	1
.01 Zap	0.01		.01	1/10

11.3 State Money Gold, silver, energy specifications

We mix in the gold and silver for legality purposes. Also, we mix in only enough so that the coins are not rounded up and melted. These coins can be limited. They can be made similar to poker chips.

Each coin has an RFID identifier, and could add some smart card properties. Each State can have its own.

There is a US State that retained some power in its money system. North Dakota is one of the only States that does not have a fiscal deficit and its unemployment rate is half of the national average. North Dakota has a State Bank that acts in many ways like the Federal Reserve. This bank supports other banks and funding sources in the State. It supports fractional reserve banking but for the interest of the population. It provides four key support roles.

- Student Loans for college students in the State.
- Lending Services that promote local agriculture, commerce and industry. These promote trade, and assists with disaster relief and fluctuations. Most loans are done through local banks, with the support of the Bank of North Dakota.
- Treasury Services. Supports municipal bond issues in the State.
- Banking Services. It acts as a Correspondent Bank for most banks in North Dakota. It guarantees the deposits.

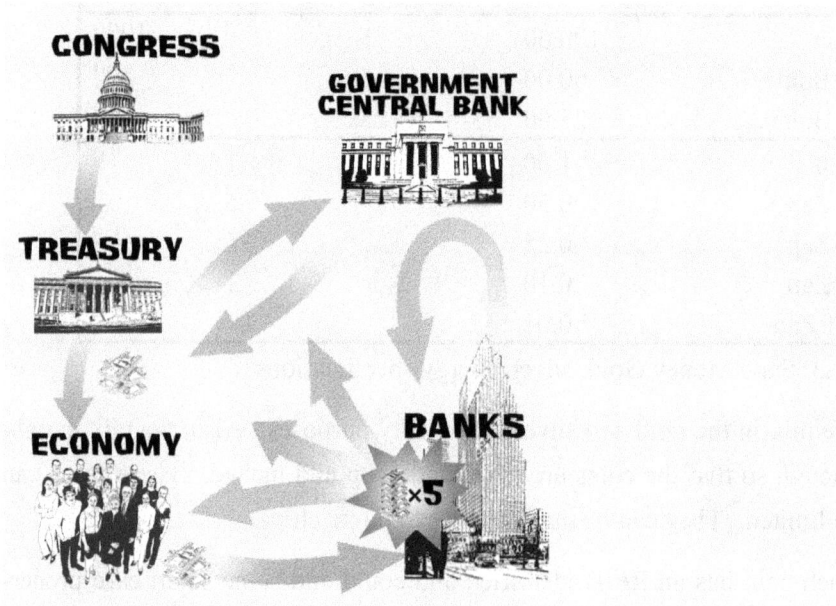

11.4 Banking System - States

The state owned bank acts in many ways like the Federal Reserve. It takes

State tax revenue and using fractional reserve it can issue loans to the residents of the state. The State Bank earns interest on its own credit. State owned banks can build infrastructure and stimulate tax revenue. The process would work something Figure 15.1. There is no banker middleman to touch the money and charge interest forever against the taxpayer. This is how North Dakota does it with its State owned bank.

It is also how China does it with its State owned bank, the People's Bank of China. China has no national debt and it is able to offer interest free loans to its exporters. When China wants to build a huge national rail network, it issues money against the project itself. It borrows from itself, and not from a private central bank. When China wants to take over a market, such as cell phones, or solar panels, it issued interest free loans.

According to the Flow of Funds statements, there is 2 trillion dollars worth of pensions in State and Local governments. Most of this money is invested in bonds and other Federal Reserve dollar denominated assets. If the dollar collapses, these funds will go away in a puff of smoke. Most states have tens of billions in pensions and they can start with five billion dollars from the pension fund. Take the pension money out of Citibank or JP Morgan, and set it up in a State Bank. With fractional reserve banking, they can leverage this five billion out to tens of billion in loans.

Let's develop a scenario that gets broad participation with homeowners and businesses. The end result will be a new asset for investments and the spreading of Power Currency in the State. Let's say we have 6 million people, and 2 million homes and small businesses in the State. Add to this all the land, farms, entrepreneurs and other opportunities. We could also consider all the unemployed people as an untapped resource. We decide to fund new factories, high speed rail, light rail, bio-fuel plants, and return some of the money to strengthen the pension funds.

people	Loan per person
10,000	100,000
90,000	10,000
900,000	5,000
1,000,000	0

Half the people will not do, and most of the rest will do just a bit. Five percent of the eligible people will take advantage of this in a big way. It's up to the person, not State coercion. If the programs are attractive, people will invest. It is similar to the participation now with people insulating homes or putting solar panels on their rooftops. The capital cost for building power plants ranges from 500 to 4000 dollars per KWH. Gas powered plants are $600/KWH, wind is about $1200/KWH, and solar thermal is about $4000/KWH now. You will need to add in funds for transmission and some extra money to grease the system and ongoing funds. As the projects develop scale, we can expect the costs to decrease. We will use 2,500 dollars per KWH for an average Capital Cost.

Out of the five billion in assets, the state will issue 6.4 billion in money credit.

People who do this	Money each borrows	Capital Cost/ KWH	KW Ca- pacity /person	Total KW per group	Money needed
10,000	100,000	2,500	40	400,000	1,000,000,000
90,000	10,000	2,500	4	360,000	900,000,000
900,000	5,000	2,500	2	1,800,000	4,500,000,000
1,000,00 0	0	2,500	0	0	
		KWH		2,560,000	6,400,000,000
		GWH		2.56	6.4 Billion

With fractional reserve, it still has well over 30 billion it can issue in credit to pay for the construction, operations. This money will circulate among the new producers and consumers driven by loans made to homeowners, farms, and businesses. Since the production of the energy is to be done on

State land, the risk level is very low. As the credit money is made from thin air and backed by public resources, the State could finance this at one or two percent interest. Here is what the payments would amount to at two percent:

Loan	2% 60 months	2% 120 months	2% 240 months
100,000	$1,752.78	$920.13	$505.88
10,000	$175.28	$92.01	$50.59
5,000	$87.64	$46.01	$25.29

The assets are secured. As the loans are paid back, the debt based money is replaced with production based energy. In exchange for the monthly payments, the people receive kilowatt hours.

Loan	KWH capacity	KWH per day	cost per KWH	value per day	value per month
100,000	40	160	$ 0.12	$ 19.20	$ 576.00
10,000	4	16	$ 0.12	$ 1.92	$ 57.60
5,000	2	8	$ 0.12	$ 0.96	$ 28.80

Much of the loan payment is a sort of tax, as most of the interest will go into the State Treasury. Even at just two percent, the State Bank would earn a decent return. On a ten year loan for ten thousand dollars, it would earn 1,041 dollars. Taking into account fractional reserve banking, they could loan out nine or ten times the amount of money in the bank, so for ten thousand, they could earn back another ten thousand dollars in interest.

It is secure. The lender can give low rate loans as they will have the means to seize the asset if the payments are not made. They could grab the energy income stream, or the asset itself.

Under this scenario, there is a lot of flexibility. Repayment is done in dollars or part of the kilowatt output. With inflation and technology advances, we will see the value of the energy more than the loan payment. This will be a sound investment for anyone. In this way, the money supply is brought back in line and replaced with producing assets.

Using this same model, we can finance production and sales of electric vehicles, mass transit and other projects. If there is a Constitutional question about the nature of the money, then just keep it purely as an investment vehicle.

The State Bank could set up a mechanism to guarantee the energy payments, and to extinguish the loan amounts as the payments in energy come into the system. The State can convert the debts into energy units and clear out the credit money. Eventually, this converts the money from debt based to non-debt based money.

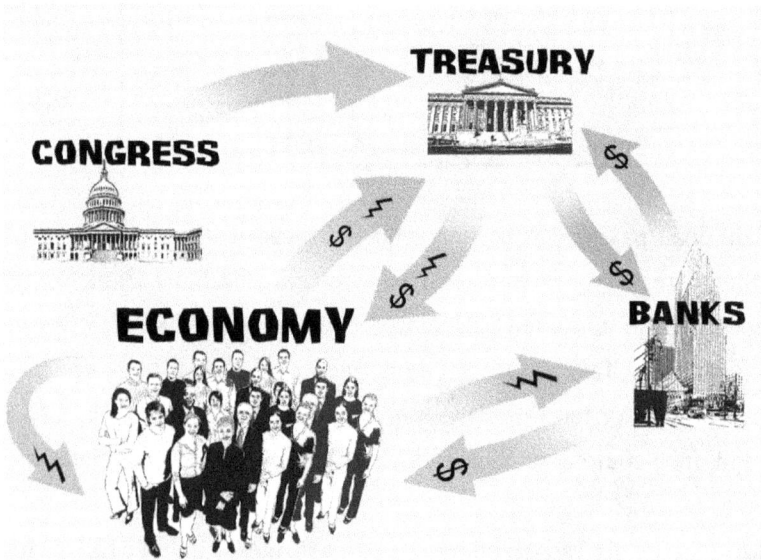

11.5 Free Market Economy with Power Currency

With this process, the money production function gets spread out to the population at large. This is the best method of all and is similar to the method set up by George Washington and Congress in 1792. Back then, the people would bring silver and gold to the mint to be coined. How they found the metals, or earned them was up to the individual. The government was there to simply mint the coins and make sure that all coins were exactly the same weight and composition as the others. So the process looks like this:

Now, instead of bringing gold or silver to the mint, people bring energy production to the utility.

Each State has its own resources – solar, biomass, wind, hydro. A State like Pennsylvania that is opening new natural gas fields can use this as collateral to finance thousands of small solar, wind, and electric vehicles.
States with distressed real estate can use some form of this to support refinancing with low interest loans tacked on with their mortgages. The guarantee is to cover existing electricity and some gas.

With this system, States can fill the budget gap with state issued scrip backed by energy. This comes from gas and future increase in electricity production via wind and coal. Communities can use this mechanism to attract companies. They issue a guarantee production deal that will ensure a steady production and sale of solar PV, solar thermal and wind generating equipment over 10 years, with more to follow. With a goal to 'go green' at two percent per year and then to add more after that they are able to guarantee 10,000 new jobs, land grants or concessions for manufacturers, etc... Then they add incentives that buildings need to install building integrated solar systems, rooftop systems and wind and CHP. Some of the new manufacturing will get financed by pension money, and payback is guaranteed at a fixed rate. The companies will be able to earn the profits above that level assuming they reinvest a certain amount per year into further development.

Other scenarios like this can be used with state pension plans. The pension fund allows workers to invest in renewable energy and receive their pension payment part in USD and part in KWH. People invest between one percent and 25 percent of their pension money into this plan as the money is allowed to grow over time by the time they hit retirements they are looking at more than enough energy for their own needs. They sell off excess to their neighbors or allow it to accrue in their account. They can buy coffee, food, clothes and whatever they want with the extra energy backed money. State pension funds can match contributions from the loan interest we mentioned above.

Some States are setting targets for new energy production across the board. Pennsylvania's "25 by 25" sets a goal for the year 2025 - 25 percent of electricity sales by renewable energy and 25 percent share of motor fuel are by renewable resources. But why do states insist on asking money from the Feds. They can move forward. With a State currency, internal, backed by State assets, they can make things happen. We could have the following

    2020. 50 percent increase in the installed capacity of electricity. 25 percent of new car sales will be plug-in hybrids and a further 20 percent of all used cars will have been converted to hybrid or plug-in hybrid.

    2025. 100 percent increase in installed capacity. Zero oil imports.

    2030. 200 percent increase in installed capacity. 90 percent of new car sales are plug-in hybrid with most of the rest using some sort of renewable liquid fuel. No imported oil.

State taxes can be paid with locally produced energy. All the production and payment is within the state, so it will not interfere with the Commerce clause.

A State like Michigan has many skilled people who are unemployed. The State can set up a fund that supports manufacturing and power generation.

Or they provide land for this purpose and subsidize the output. Then they encourage businesses to purchase part of their energy from this system. This will add to the economy as the seller of electricity is earning income which they will reinvest. They can set up system where the company will earn tax breaks if they reinvest profits back into the renewable energy field and hire local citizens. Adopting a power currency system can help both employers and the employees to negotiate better labor contracts, and find a win-win for everyone.

Cities and counties can tie in new development efforts with property taxes. People have an option to buy into a town sponsored wind farm coop. The buy in allows people to make a small capital investment into the farm then get paid back in KWH cash. Through revitalization campaigns, residents are able to put energy systems in their homes that are produced locally. The town is able to finance the placement of 5,000 units installed over a period of time. Then some vacant lots and deteriorating warehouses and homes are turned over to small bio-fuel refineries and power plants. This then burns off some of the waste from the residents feeding this heat and electricity back into the local grid. This could easily handle 20 percent of the energy needs of the town. Furthermore, the investors are able to see a return on their investment in the form of cash, energy credits and the increased value of the land. The local government also wins with higher tax collections.

Universities can set up funding mechanisms. Parents buy into the energy with the savings plans. Then they pay tuition in the future with amounts on order of 10 MW per year, fixed. The invested amount goes into wind farms, and micro grids. Students earn credits for doing things for the community, care for the elderly, etc... The schools can set aside a quota of 5 percent or so to cash in these currency units. Online education communities can use Power Currency to facilitate barter. The professors can accept money in LETS hours, Federal Reserve debt money, or Power Currency. The students can pay likewise.

Scenario – Year 2030.

As coal fired plants age, they are shut down. The downtown area has one million square feet of commercial office space and power systems they use an array of distributed resources. The area buildings fill up on energy during early morning hours and place this potential into banks of flywheels, batteries and other storage. Vehicles in the parking lot can plug in and help with peak load, base load or even sell their KWH to neighboring buildings. The hybrid cars can turn on engines and feed power right into the local grid and work as an emergency generators in times of blackout, or unusual peak demand. As an added benefit, this system also will provide a significant benefit to the City distribution grid by reducing load on the grid during the critical summer peak hours. It plans to tie in the parking garage so that BEV and PHEV can offload KWH of energy during peak times. This energy will be paid back to the customer in credits. The office town pulled in their parking garage to installs a system for pulling KWH from the cars and selling to the local buildings. The garage has 1000 slots, 400 of which are able to pull in KWH. In exchange for 10KWH, they reduce the price of parking by half. This provides 4 MWH per cay - 400 x 10 KWH - during peak times.

The town has developed more than enough energy for its own needs. They have three GWH generating capacity. From this they use one GWH; they export and sell one GWH capacity, which brings in millions of dollars to its tax base, and use the other GWH as incentives. The residents who bought into the coop get dividends and rebates from this as well as eliminating their power bill. Due to recent economic changes, the town decided to attract companies with high wage jobs with very attractive rates to the company on power, subsidies and land use. The city issues bonds backed and guaranteed by the MWH sales contracts that it has developed with buyers. These bonds are used for infrastructure, arts, and general welfare.

CHINA'S AMERICAN SYSTEM

The American System was a plan to strengthen and unify the nation. The interstate highway system was the last great project built under this type of system. An integrated high speed rail system could be next.

The American System was an economic plan based on the "American School" ideas of Alexander Hamilton. It consisted of a high tariff to support internal improvements such as road-building, and a national bank to encourage productive enterprise with a national currency. This program was intended to allow the United States to grow and prosper, by providing a defense against the dumping of cheap foreign products from the British Empire.

The American System was the dominant economic system in 19th Century USA. It strengthened the country, protected innovation and allowed a strong middle class to develop. It built out our country to be the leading

147

power in the world by 1920. This system is now strongly rejected by the powers in charge of our money system.

The elements of the American System included:
- Support for a high tariff to protect American industries and generate revenue for the federal government
- Maintenance of high public land prices to generate federal revenue
- Preservation of the Bank of the United States to stabilize the currency and rein in risky state and local banks
- Infrastructure such as roads, canals, dams that would tie the country together and be financed by land sales and tariffs.

An example of this system was the transcontinental railway which started to be built during the Civil War. The Pacific Railway Act was passed on July 1, 1862. It provided Federal subsidies in land and loans for the construction of a transcontinental railroad across the United States. Congress set aside huge amounts of land for this. The United States understood that rail was a lot more than about delivery of people and goods. It opened new areas of the country for settlement, and farming. The rail system was a huge accomplishment for the leaders who advocated the American System.

Lincoln pushed the railway system though and was racing to get back to a commodity backed money system. His plans were to get off of the emergency debt system and back to a gold and silver standard. He saw the opening of the West as the salvation of the country. Shortly before he died Lincoln had a conversation the Speaker of the House, Schuyler Colfax.

> Mr. Colfax, I want you to take a message from me to the miners whom you visit. I have very large ideas of the mineral wealth of our nation. I believe it practically inexhaustible. It abounds all over the Western country, from the Rocky Mountains to the Pacific, and its development has scarcely commenced. During the war,

when we were adding a couple of millions of dollars every day to our national debt, I did not care about encouraging the increase in the volume of our precious metals. We had the country to save first. But now that the rebellion is overthrown, and we know pretty nearly the amount of our national debt, the more gold and silver we mine, we make the payment of that debt so much the easier. "Now," said he, speaking with more emphasis, "I am going to encourage that in every possible way. We shall have hundreds of thousands of disbanded soldiers, and many have feared that their return home in such great numbers might paralyze industry, by furnishing, suddenly, a greater supply of labor than there will be demand for. I am going to try to attract them to the hidden wealth of our mountain ranges, where there is room enough for all. Immigration, which even the war has not stopped, will land upon our shores hundreds of thousands more per year from overcrowded Europe. I intend to point them to the gold and silver that wait for them in the West. Tell the miners for me, that I shall promote their interests to the utmost of my ability; because their prosperity is the prosperity of the nation; and," said he, his eye kindling with enthusiasm, "we shall prove, in a very few years, that we are indeed the treasury of the world."

Schuyler was the Speaker of the House when Lincoln was assassinated and was to become the Vice President under Ulysses Grant[xii].

Punahoe High School in Hawaii can boast having had two Presidents - President Barack Obama, and President of China Sun Yatsen. Today in China, Sun is revered. His portrait is prominently displayed during the 60th birthday celebrations.

Sun Yatsen had great respect for President Lincoln. He was inspired by Abraham Lincoln and said:

> "A government of the people, elected by the people and for the people." These principles have served as the maximum of achievement for Europeans as well as Americans. Words which have the same sense can be found in China: I have translated them: "nationalism, democracy and socialism." Of course, there can be other interpretations. The wealth and power of the United States are a striking example of the results of great men's teachings in that country. I am glad to observe that my principles, too, are shared by the greatest political minds abroad and are not in contradiction to all the world's democratic schools of thought."
> http://www.milestonedocuments.com/documents/full-text/sun-yat-sensthe-three-principles-of-the-people

In particular he looked at how the USA developed their intercontinental railroads. After establishing the Republic Sun focused on strategic plans for the future. In 1921 Sun Yatsen wrote a strategic plan for the development of China, 'The International Development of China'. He invited countries to invest and build out China's ports, railroads, highways and manufacturing capabilities.

He planned a rail network that would link China's princes and tie in with Central Asia, Russia, and India. He invited the United States to help China to develop into a strong trade partner. This would create a huge market for their goods, and open up production that would help the world. This comprehensive plan was interrupted by war and famine, and had to wait a few decades. The plan is going full steam ahead now.

China adopts the American System.

There are many stories in the business press about China copying American technology and products, movies, ideas, etc.. The biggest thing that China copied from American was the successful American System. Today the United States abandoned the American System, and China uses the American System. Of course, the Communist leaders will say they use Marxist theory, Lenin concepts, Mao thought, Deng theory and all that lovely stuff. Today, China uses the same concepts as the American System:

- Support for a high tariff to protect Chinese industries and generate revenue for the national government.
- Maintenance of high public land prices to generate tax revenue.
- Preservation of the People's Bank of China to stabilize the currency and rein in risky state and local banks
- Infrastructure such as train networks, ports, roads, power grids, dams that would tie the country together and be financed by land sales and tariffs.

China is building a world class high speed network. The overall plan is to have a vast network that will connect all provincial capitals, and most of the top 250 cities. Already they have linked Beijing with Tianjin with a non-stop 30 minute ride. The trains run full, and have done a lot more than deliver people between the two cities. It has also spurred a real estate boom that is helping to pay for the railway. Large tracts of land have been sold to pay for much of the project, while other concessions have been sold. Property values have more than doubled in the last five years stimulating the economy. Distribution between the cities is no longer impeded by old overused highways. New businesses are popping up. More than 2 Trillion RMB (about 300 billion USD) has been allocated for the project. All this money is issued debt free. The money is issued against the project itself, and as the project will add so much production to the economy, it is self funding and non-inflationary. The potential for high speed transport and distribution will multiply their GDP and pay off the rail system many times over.

One key element of the American System is a Central Bank that issues non-debt national currency. China was on a debt based fiat money system in the 1920's through the 1940's. Eventually, the money inflated and collapsed. The money increased exponentially and was issued by a privately controlled Central Bank. Now, China issues its own money debt free, and has no national debt. Money Supply in China is driven by production. Just as mining for gold and silver in the good old days, China drives their money supply through bring metals, energy, and building materials out of the ground. Below you can see that the supply of money has risen 12 percent per year for M0 and a much higher rate for M1 and M2.

	M0	M1	M2	Metals	Industry
2004				23	185
2005				32	222
2006	45	280	699	47	292
2007	49	396	863	56	341
2008	57	204	1071	60	391
2009	60	803	1956	65*	475*

12.1 China Money Supply * estimate

Source: People's Bank of China, usgs.gov

Increase in Money supply year on year, compared to mining of select minerals[xiii]

Metals: Gold, Silver, Copper, Nickel, Tin, Titanium, Tungsten, Zinc, Rare Earth, Lead, Magnesium, Manganese, Molybdenum, Vanadium

Industry: Cement, Aluminum, Iron Ore, Coal

The primary metals mining and industry, have kept pace with this growth in money. The amount of major metals mined is about equal to the increase in money in circulation. The value for Industrial materials such as

Cement, Iron, Aluminum and Coal has kept pace with the added M1. If you add in all the land sales, value added activities and the huge increase in foreign reserves, we can see that production supports the money supply.

Energy prospects in China.

China also aims to be energy independent. China takes the energy situation as a national strategic issue to be fixed and is using its large State Own enterprises and Military to fix it. They are building huge wind farms in China. They are developing solutions in hybrid vehicles, and battery technology. They are copying some of the R&D that the USA has done with hybrid electric vehicles. China will adopt the electric and PHEV car. They are not beholden to big oil and even their big energy companies are not locked into oil.

The adoption rate of new things goes very fast. If production in China takes off for solar and wind like it did for cell phones and computer components, then the energy game will change. China is world class at mass manufacturing. They build, build and build then the people buy. Here is the growth chart for wind energy in China. Similar style charts exist for car production, mobile phones, internet, and other products.

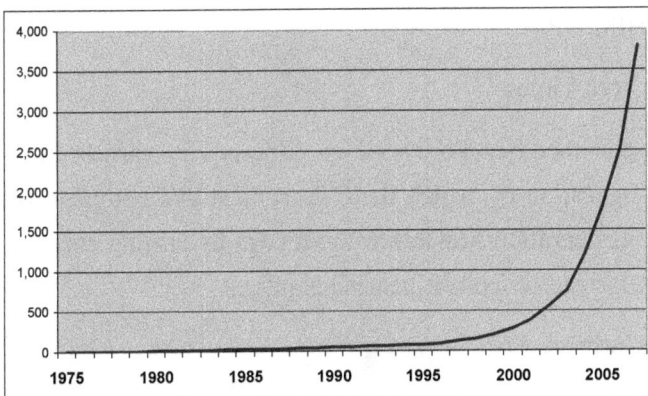

12.2 Wind in China

It is quite possible that the electric car is China's entry into the US car

153

market. They have the lead with electric bikes and scooters and three wheelers and are moving into the car market soon. An electric car that is fun to use and passes the crash test could win over the US car market. In the near future China builds millions of electric cars each year. GM China goes along with this, Toyota goes along with this. If the big auto companies don't get on board, we will have a situation as in the UK where all the big homegrown auto manufacturers are wiped out.

Ford and Edison

Henry Ford and Thomas Edison saw the nature of the money problem when the Federal Reserve's intentions were first exposed. The media could still report negatively against the nature of the debt money system. Imagine if they could only see our money system now that is built upon thin air. They give a very logical argument against usury and for the government to issue debt free money to support production.

Here is an article from the New York Time December 6, 1921.
FORD SEES WEALTH IN MUSCLE SHOALS

Says Development Will Bring Great Prosperity to That Section of the South

EDISON BACKS HIM UP

Special to the New York Times

Thomas A. Edison endorsed Mr. Ford's views.... he is very earnest in his support of Ford's suggestion by which the Government can complete the property and make its operation possible without cost, by issuing currency against the property instead of interest-bearing bonds....

Support for Ford's Currency Plan

On the point of Mr. Ford's suggestion to the Government for financing the completion of the dam, Mr. Edison reiterated his belief that it was a good plan and that if only the currency method is tried in raising money for public improvements, this country will never go back to the borrowing method.

"Make it perfectly clear that I'm not advocating any changes in banks and banking," said Mr. Edison. "Banks are a mighty good thing. They are essential to the commerce of the country. It is the money broker, the money profiteer, the private banker that I oppose. They gain their power through a fictitious and false value given to gold.

"Gold is a relic of Julius Caesar and interest is an invention of Satan," Mr. Edison continued. "Gold is intrinsically of less utility than most metals. The probable reason why it is retained as the basis of money is that it is easy to control. And it is the control of money that constitutes the money question. It is the control of money that is the root of all evil."

"Then there is another way—the method my friend Ford proposed the other day. He proposes just to go along and forget about gold. He says that the government can finance Muscle Shoals without applying to money brokers for permission, and I think he is absolutely right about it.

"But would not Mr. Ford's suggestion that Muscle Shoals be financed by a currency issue raised some objection?" Mr. Edison was asked.

"Certainly. There is a complete set of misleading slogans kept on hand for just such outbreaks of common sense among the people. The people are so ignorant of what they think are the intricacies of the money system that they are easily impressed by big words. There would be new shrieks of 'fiat money,' and 'paper money' and 'greenbackism,' And all the rest of it—the same old cries with which the people have been shouted down from the beginning.

"Maybe they can't shout down American thinkers any longer. The only dynamite that works in this country is the dynamite of a sound idea. I think we are getting a sound idea on the money question. The people have an instinct which tells them that something is wrong, and that the wrong somehow centers in money. They have an instinct also, which tells them when a proposal is made in their interests or against them.

"Now here is Ford proposing to finance muscle Shoals by an issue of currency. Very well, let us suppose for a moment that Congress follows his proposal. The required sum is authorized—say $30 million. The bills are issued directly by the government, as all money ought to be. When the working men are paid off they received these United States bills. When the material is blocked it is paid in these United States bills. Except that perhaps the bills may have the engraving of a water dam, instead of a railroad train and a ship, as some of the Federal Reserve notes have. They will be the same as any other currency put out by the government; that is, they will be money. They will be based on the public wealth already in Muscle Shoals, and their circulation will increase that public wealth, not only the public money but the public wealth—real wealth.

"When these bills have answered the purpose of building and completing Muscle Shoals, they will be retired by the earnings of the power dam. That is, the people of the United States will have all that they put into Muscle Shoals and all that they can take out for centuries—the endless wealth making water power of the great Tennessee River—with no tax and no increase of the national debt."

But suppose Congress does not see this, what then?" Mr. Edison was asked.

"Well, Congress must fall back on the old way of doing business. It must authorize an issue of bonds. That is, it must go out to the money brokers and borrow enough of our own national currency to complete great national resources, and we then must pay interest of the money brokers for the

"That is to say, under the old way any time we wish to add to the national wealth we are compelled to add to the national debt.

"Now, that is what Henry Ford wants to prevent. He thinks it is stupid, and so do I, but for the loan of $30 million of their own money to people of the United States should be compelled to pay $66 million—that is what it amounts to, with interest. People who will not turn a shovel full of dirt nor

156

contribute a pound of material will collect more money from the United States than will the people who supply the material and do the work. That is the terrible thing about interest. In all our great bond issues the interest is always greater than the principal. All of the great public Works cost more than twice the actual cost, on that account. Under the present system of doing business we simply add 120 to 150 percent to the stated cost.

"But here's the point: if our nation can issue a dollar bond, it can issue a dollar bill. The element that makes the bond good makes the bill good, also. The difference between the bond and the bill is that the bond lets the money brokers collect twice the amount of the bond and an additional 20%, whereas the currency pays nobody but those who directly contribute to Muscle Shoals in some useful way.

"It is absurd to say that our country can issue $30 million in bonds and not $30 million in currency. Both are promises to pay; but one promised fattens the usurer, and the other helps the people. If the currency issued by the government were no good than the bonds issued would be no good either. It is a terrible situation when the government, to increase the national wealth, must go into debt and submit to ruinous interest charges at the hands of men who control the fictitious values of gold.

"Look at it another way. If the government issues bonds, the brokers will sell them. The bonds will be negotiable; they will be considered as gilt-edged paper. Why? Because the government is behind them, but who is behind the government? The people. Therefore it is the people who constitute the basis of government credit. Why then cannot the people have the benefit of their own gilt-edged credit by receiving non-interest-bearing currency on Muscle Shoals, instead of the bankers and receiving the benefit of the people's credit in interest-bearing bonds?"

"The people must pay anyway; why should they be compelled to pay twice, as the bonded system compels them to pay? The people of the United States always accept the government's currency. If the United States government will adopt this policy of increasing its national wealth without contributing to the interest collector—for the whole national debt is made up of interest charges—then you will see an era of progress and prosperity in this country such as could never have come otherwise."

Let's apply Edison and Ford's views in light of China and the USA.

USURY SYSTEM	AMERICAN SYSTEM
America 21st Century Company needs to borrow 500 million for solar production plant and equipment	**China 21st Century** Company needs to borrow 500 million for solar production plant and equipment
Borrows money at 5 percent interest and pays extensive environmental fees and overhead	Borrows money at 0 percent interest, with low costs and overhead
Sells solar cells at 4 dollars per watt (1 dollar to interest and 1 dollar to extra costs). 20 cents profit per watt	Sells solar cells at 2 dollars per watt. 20 cents profit per watt - same as American company
Cant compete with China price	Chinese company sells products and expands
Collectivists confiscate homes of workers who lost their jobs and can't pay their mortgage	Chinese company buys American company with Chinese Government backed funds or puts American company out of business

12.3 China's American System vs America's Usury System

It is pretty absurd, but there it is.

ENERGY HOMESTEADS

Congress has the power to take over the Federal Reserve and to issue debt free money. It can issue this money against the credit of the United States and does not need to hand this awesome power over to some small group of banks.

Western Lands Energy Homesteads

Much of the American West was founded by settlers who claimed land and set up homesteads. The Homestead Acts of 1862, 1909 and 1916 gave settlers an opportunity to gain title to federal land. The law required people to improve the land and after five years file for the deed. Eventually 1.6 million homesteads were granted and 420 thousand square miles of federal land were privatized between 1862 and 1934.

We can do the same now with energy.

According to the National Renewable Energy Laboratory, a 100 mile by 100 mile plot of land in the Southwest USA, fitted with solar energy systems, could provide enough electricity for the entire United States.

Looking at the 100 mile by 100 mile plot of land gives us 6.4 million acres. The Bureau of Land Management manages 245 million surface acres of US land. Just a small part of this is enough space to build enough energy projects to increase our energy wealth many times over. This would kill the dependence on oil imports, support transportation projects and support millions of new full time jobs.

Now, the BLM supports all sorts of oil, gas and coal production. Over five billion dollars is collected each year from royalties – half goes to the State, and half to the Federal Government - reducing the need for income taxes. The BLM is spending $41 million for 65 projects to test production of re-newable energy on their lands. These lands are ideal for tapping into wind, solar, geothermal and biomass potential. Alternative liquid fuels are also made from waste products or switch grass.

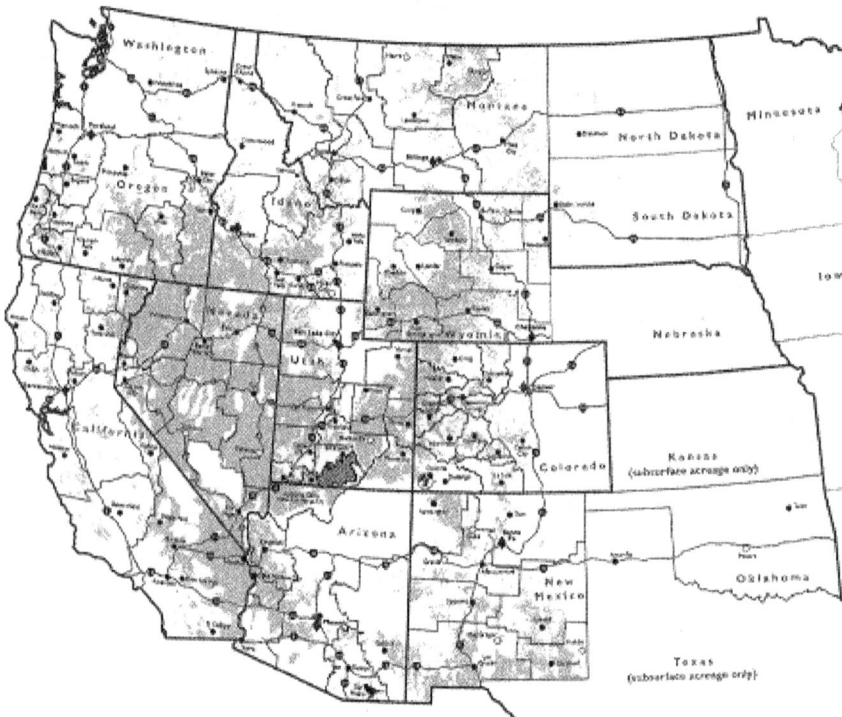

13.1 Bureau of Land Management – US Public Lands

Looking at the map you can see that the lands are in the Western USA with a great deal of that in the sunny Southwest desert.

	Current Projects	MWH
Solar	14	3572
Wind	29	800
Geothermal	41	1585

Here we set up a system for energy homesteads. Let's use a solar project as a benchmark. In 2006, Acciona Energy built a Concentrated Solar thermal project in the Nevada desert 40 miles from Las Vegas. This uses parabolic troughs and started operation in 2007.

Size: 64 MW

Land area: 400 acres

Cost: 266 million dollars

Electricity Generation: 134,000 MWH/yr

Construction Job Years   350

Annual Operation and Maintenance Jobs: 30

Based on this, we generate the following numbers

4,156 dollars per KWH cap cost

2,093 KWH per year per KWH installed capacity

23.9 percent utilization.

We allow for storage, roads, transmission and other land. Let's say that one square mile, or 640 acres, for a 64 MWH plant. 400 acres are for the power, and 240 for access roads, storage and extra support.

We can project that the unit cost will drop as we do mass production. After 50 plants are built, we can get the cost down to 2000 dollars per KWH, and after 250 plants we can get the cost down to 1000 dollars per KWH. We allocate 10 percent of the energy output to pay for ongoing operations and dividends for the investors.

Right now the BLM leases 45 million acres for drilling and mining. Of this 45 million, 11.7 are managed and only 472,000 acres are directly disturbed by oil and gas activity. Solar and wind each have 20 million acres of potential within the BLM lands so we do not have a land problem.

Acres	472,000	2,000,000
% of BLM lands	0.2%	0.8%
Square Miles	737	3,125
64MWH/mile	47,200	200,000
MWH/year	98,825,000	418,750,000
Construction jobs	258,125	1,093,750
O&M jobs	22,125	93,750

The first scenario matches the amount of land that is disturbed by coal mining, and oil & gas drilling. This one would increase our energy supply 2.5 percent while adding over a quarter million jobs. Think how much imported oil we could displace, and the amount of money that gets circulated within the community. The second scenario would use only ten percent of the BLM land that is suitable for solar energy. This would give us enough renewable energy for all cars to go electric. If you are into the global warming propaganda, it would displace scores of coal plants and save a kajillion tons of CO_2. It would increase the total USA energy output over ten percent, while providing over one million jobs.

POWER CURRENCY

Offshore Wind Energy Homesteads

Along the Atlantic seaboard there are a number of offshore wind farms in the planning stage. These all seem to be stuck in bureaucratic red tape. Offshore wind is a proven technology in Europe. Already five countries have built more than 100 MWH or offshore wind capacity.

> United Kingdom more than 1300 MWH
>
> Denmark more than 800 MWH
>
> Netherlands more than 200 MWH
>
> Belgium more than 150 MWH
>
> Sweden more than 100 MWH

There are thousands of MWH being constructed now and tens of thousands of MWH being planned. These projects cost more to build, but are far less complex than offshore drilling rigs. Technically there is not a problem. There are a lot of advantages to offshore wind. It is pretty much out of sight. The wind is steadier, so you get more energy. Undersea power transmission cables can get up to the large coastal cities, taking pressure off the need to build new ugly above ground transmission towers.

Right now the projects are all being financed with debt backed money, so ultimately a lot of the money will go back to the shareholders of the Federal Reserve. Instead of that, the Government can issue the money debt free and charge zero to two percent financing. Any interest into the Treasury can be used for general revenue and to offset income taxes.

Let's set up a scenario here. We plan to build 1000 MWH capacity of wind farms. Each MWH will average out to 5000 dollars, so the project costs five billion dollars. The US Government issues five billion in debt free money. They charge one percent interest on this money, and that money goes back to the Treasury to cover some other expenses, like healthcare for the contractors, admin, insider dealings and so forth. Let's look at it here comparing US backed non-debt money to Federal Reserve Bank debt money.

	Federal Reserve Notes	US Treasury money
Capital cost per MWH	4.6 million	4.6 million
Ongoing costs per MWH	0.4 million	0.4 million
MWH	1,000	1,000
Capital cost total	5 billion	5 billion
loan	5 billion	5 billion

Interest Rate	Five percent	One percent
Monthly payment 20 Year Loan	32,997,787	22,994,715
Total Payments	7,919,468,871	5,518,731,683
Interest	2,919,468,871	518,731,683
Where the interest goes:	All to the banks lending the US its own credit	Back to the treasury

Using US Treasury money, the interest payments go back to the Treasury. Someone needs to ultimately pay for that interest cost, so we might as well use it to reduce taxes.

There is another way to look at this. This added interest cost adds four cents to every kilowatt hour that is produced - forever.

per month KWH[xiv]	246,575,342	246,575,342
Monthly payment	32,997,787	22,994,715
Cost per KWH/monthly payment	0.13	0.09
Difference		0.04

This is four cents purely from paying interest to the bankers at five percent as opposed to paying one percent interest for government backed debt. Remember, this money lent by the Wankers is made from thin air. This four cents extra on each KWH would work its way through the economy. The baker, retailer, and producer all need to pass on this extra four cents (or about 30 percent) onto the next person.

Now, if you have a choice, what would you choose?

The government could issue the money, and let one big utility do all the work and then set a certain fee for all output. This is the way we accept as normal in 2010.

Or there is the third way. This is an ideal project to use for US issued debt free money converted into Power Currency.

The financing for this is carried out among people who choose to participate. As people buy new electric or hybrid electric cars, they have the option to buy a slice of production of the project.

> New car owners - 200 thousand owners finance 2 billion
> Car conversions - 50 thousand finance 500 million
> New homes - 100 thousand finance 600 million
> Distressed homes - 100 thousand finance 600 million
> Government, Investors, Other finance 1.3 billion.
> Total is 5 billion.

Here is a breakdown for a new car sale. Someone buys a new electric or hybrid car. That car needs 400 watts per mile. They buy a package that gives them 15000 miles over the next forty years, which is the expected life of the wind turbine. This is financed for the first twenty years and the second twenty years is all theirs to keep.

15000 miles X 400 watts per mile is 6000 KWH need each year, or 500 each month.

6000 KWH needs 2 KWH capacity

Each KWH of capacity costs 5000 dollars, so they will need a loan for 10,000 dollars.

Using a 20 year loan at one percent interest, we get monthly payments of 46 dollars.

500 KWH each month costing 12 cents is worth 60 dollars so they have a nice 14 dollar benefit there. As electricity prices go up in the future, this benefit increases.

So in this deal, the new car owner would have a monthly payment of 46 dollars over the next twenty years, as opposed to 60 dollars. Any KWH the car owner does not use is used as money in the form of Power Currency. Any time the owner is short of KWH in any month, he can buy from the electric grid.

This is a better system than taxation. It would stir the market and provide the financing. Compare this to the current situation where money is hard to raise and there are all sorts of hands in the cookie jar.

Now the government taxes you, then borrows from the Federal Reserve and adds to the national debt. Finally, they come back to you to pay the interest on the national debt. The government says they will issue grants to research and development for developing the turbines and other items. That grant money comes from the budget which must be borrow from the banks, and back to the debt which ultimately is paid by the taxpayer. At all points, there is debt and taxes.

A better way is to have public works projects that are privately financed. The government can provide a support for the private economy instead of the private economy supporting bureaucrats and usurers. This can also be done with homeowners. They use the same calculations we went through with cars. You replace miles with home energy use and bundle the payment in with the mortgage payment.

Distressed real estate can use this. Take property where the mortgage is more than the home is worth. Now most of those properties are on the government's books but with the interest payments still go to the share-holders of the Federal Reserve. In this case the beneficiaries are Citigroup, JP Morgan, Goldman Sachs, Wells Fargo and Bank of America.

We could convert a lot of debt Federal Reserve money over to US money right away. In 2009, there was a huge jump in the Assets and Liabilities of the FED (see table 6.17). This explosion of the financial system came from the bubbles bursting and the crash in 2008. Assets and liabilities more than doubled in 2008. This was the financial crisis. There is a lot of detail here and the Federal Reserve Bank has made strong efforts not to release the details of the transactions.

The banks were able to shift their bad loans over to the Federal Reserve, and onto the taxpayer. The Agency and GSE backed securities are companies like Fannie Mae and Freddie Mac. The bad loans that were on the books of the banks like Bank of America, Wells Fargo, Citibank and JP Morgan Chase, were shifted over to Fannie Mae and Freddie Mac.

Then those bad assets were shifted to the Fed's balance sheet. Also, notice in table 6.17 how the Federal Reserve increased the bank reserves of those banks from 20 billion in 2007 to 860 billion in 2008. It's great if you can be in this industry and twist arms and get laws passed that transfer 800 billion dollars over to your balance sheet. The rest of us have to work for a living.

Using this energy project in conjunction with the distressed property, the government swaps out the mortgage note to a US Government debt free based note that charges one percent interest. Then they add in some of the energy production on top, and wrap the notes together, to make the overall note healthier. A homeowner that is upside down on their note can switch over to US Government money through US Government Fannie Mae and Freddie Mac.

	2007	2008	2009
Gold	34.2	35.71	36.18
Treasury Currency	38.68	38.67	42.69
Treasury Securities	740.61	475.92	776.59
Other	65.15	96.79	93.8
Federal Reserve Loans to Banks	48.64	**1050.1**	239.45
Foreign Currencies	24	553.73	10.27
GSE-Backed Securities	0	19.71	**1068.3**
Total Assets	951.28	2270.63	2267.22
Bank reserves	20.77	**860**	**976.99**
Vault Cash of Banks	55	57.73	54.92
Due to GSE	1.68	21.07	35.12
Federal Reserve Notes	773.94	832.17	873.33
Due to Federal Government	16.38	365.71	191.87
Other	65.07	112.87	109.35
Total Liabilities	932.84	2249.55	2241.58

6.17 Fed balance Sheet 2007 to 2009

Now: Mortgage is 250,000, Home is worth 150,000. Monthly payment at 5 percent plus taxes is 1400 per month. Electricity costs 400 per month.

Change to: Mortgage is 250,000. Reduce interest rate on mortgage. Add in zero interest financing for an energy homestead costing 50,000. Monthly payment at 2 percent for the mortgage and zero percent for the energy homestead is about 1500 per month. Electricity costs are zero as the energy comes from the Energy homestead. Home regains value over time.

Note that interest money goes to the Government coffers, and can pay for social programs - medicare and veterans benefits, for example.

TRAINGRID

Another national project we can do along these lines is a national high speed rail. Looking at the map of the USA, lets imagine a high speed rail system driven by electricity and funded by energy homesteads and Social Security taxes.

It is reasonable to build a high speed railroad linking Los Angeles to the Mississippi River (St Louis). This line could connect Vegas, Phoenix, Kansas City and have branch lines to Denver, Dallas, etc. The electricity comes from energy homesteads, independent power producers, coal plants, wind farms and solar thermal energy. This would create over one million jobs, and give us a faster transportation sector. Kansas State fans could take a Thursday overnight train to watch a basketball match with UCLA, have a great weekend, and return for class Monday morning. The transportation energy costs will be reduced by 50 percent compared to truck transportation, and time is cut in half.

The train grid integrates with the transmission lines. This power line will parallel with rail lines and shifts energy back and forth along the route and population centers. This type of grid would take some engineering and inventions. We put men on the moon, didn't we?

How to fund? The Train project is funded with United States Notes (not Federal Reserve Notes) that are backed by land, energy production and transportation. Large tracts of desert in Nevada and other States become opened to private investment through energy homesteads and big Government funding from social security payroll taxes. This investment is in the form of zero interest loans backed by national debt free currency. Repayment is in the form of power currency and United States issued money. The United States Dollars could even be backed by energy and train traffic. Social Security recipients can use this money pay their energy bills, and travel on trains. The extra money is spent into the economy. Eventually, people will redeem this money. Contractors and workers are paid in debt free currency which would drop the overall costs dramatically.

Let's take Train Grid and Social Security and see what we can develop.

"Under current law, the cost of Social Security will soon begin to increase faster than the program's income because of the aging of the baby-boom generation, expected continuing low fertility (compared to the baby-boom period), and increasing life expectancy. Based on the Trustees' best estimate, program cost will exceed tax revenues starting in 2016 and throughout the remainder of the 75-year projection period. "

Social Security Annual Report

There are various estimates regarding the future of Social Security - all predict that the system will run out of money. Some estimates say that the system will be completely bankrupt in 25 years. The Feds admit that they have spent all of the Social Security taxes they have collected over the past 70 years, and now they must pay for Social Security out of general tax revenues. In 2010, they offered no cost of living increase in benefits to account for inflation, and it is likely we will see this happen more in the future.

OASDI net cash flows as a percentage of GDP, 1957–2009, projected under the intermediate
assumptions, 2010–2085

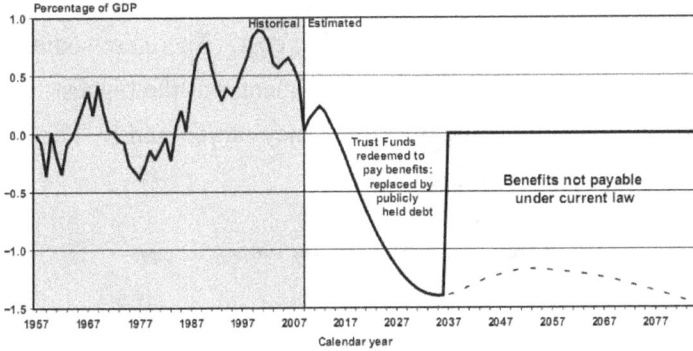

14.1 SSA Shortfall

In 2008, 900 Billion in Social Security taxes was collected, and about that much was paid out. The problem from now on is that more will be paid out than will be received in taxes. Looking at the funding gap between the retirement benefits and tax revenue, there appears an ongoing 20 percent funding gap.

Figure II.D5.—OASDI Cost and Scheduled Tax Revenue as a Percentage of GDP

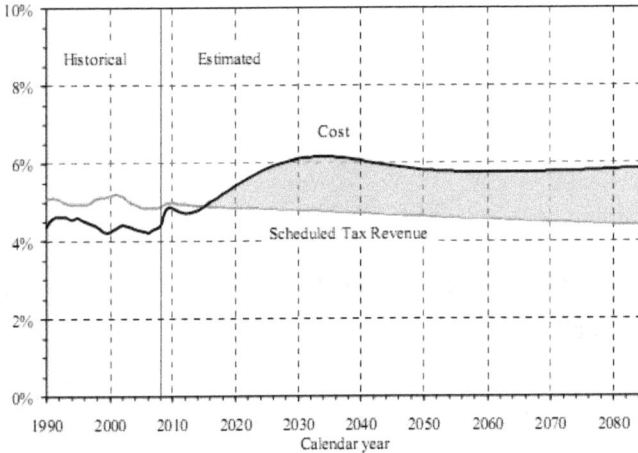

14.2 SSA Costs

From the Annual Report of the Board of Trustees of the Social Security Trust Funds we get the projections based on low, average and high costs. So what is the difference between low and high cost? There are some factors like slow economic growth, and unemployment, but the biggest 'cost' according to the bureaucrats is the life expectancy of you and I. The high cost model amounts to people living long lives.

Figure II.D6.—Long-Range OASDI Trust Fund Ratios Under Alternative Assumptions
[Assets as a percentage of annual cost]

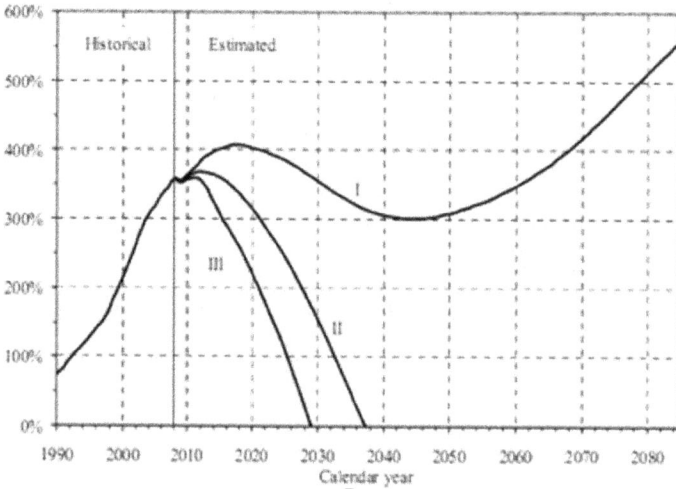

14.3 SSA - Low, Medium, High Costs

I – low cost

II – average

III – high cost.

14.3 SSA scenarios

There is a terrible conflict in motivation here. So if we live longer this is a bad thing? How about all the added wisdom that people can give to others as they live longer?

Let's put ourselves into another box. What if we decide that we are going to find a way to let people live as long as they want, don't encourage an early death, live in abundance, and cover our social security obligations?

Table V.A3.—Period Life Expectancy [a]

Calendar year	Low-cost At birth Male	Female	Low-cost At age 65 Male	Female	Intermediate At birth Male	Female	Intermediate At age 65 Male	Female	High-cost At birth Male	Female	High-cost At age 65 Male	Female
Historical data:												
1940					61.4	65.7	11.9	13.4				
1945					62.9	68.4	12.6	14.4				
1950					65.6	71.1	12.8	15.1				
1955					66.7	72.8	13.1	15.6				
1960					66.7	73.2	12.9	15.9				
1965					66.8	73.8	12.9	16.3				
1970					67.2	74.9	13.1	17.1				
1975					68.7	76.6	13.7	18.0				
1980					69.9	77.5	14.0	18.4				
1985					71.1	78.2	14.4	18.6				
1990					71.8	78.9	15.1	19.1				
1995					72.5	79.1	15.4	19.1				
1996					73.0	79.2	15.5	19.1				
1997					73.4	79.4	15.6	19.1				
1998					73.7	79.4	15.7	19.1				
1999					73.8	79.3	15.7	19.0				
2000					74.0	79.4	15.9	19.0				
2001					74.1	79.5	16.1	19.1				
2002					74.2	79.5	16.2	19.1				
2003					74.4	79.6	16.3	19.2				
2004					74.8	80.0	16.7	19.5				
2005					74.8	80.0	16.7	19.5				
2006 [b] ...					75.1	79.9	16.7	19.3				
2007 [b] ...					75.2	79.9	16.8	19.3				
2008 [b] ...					75.4	80.0	16.9	19.3				
Projected:												
2010	75.5	79.9	16.9	19.3	75.7	80.1	17.0	19.4	75.9	80.2	17.1	19.5
2015	75.8	80.0	17.1	19.3	76.4	80.5	17.4	19.6	76.9	81.0	17.8	20.0
2020	76.1	80.2	17.2	19.4	77.0	81.0	17.8	19.9	77.9	81.8	18.4	20.5
2025	76.3	80.4	17.4	19.5	77.6	81.4	18.1	20.2	78.9	82.6	19.0	21.1
2030	76.6	80.6	17.5	19.6	78.1	81.9	18.4	20.5	79.8	83.4	19.6	21.7
2035	76.8	80.8	17.6	19.7	78.6	82.4	18.7	20.8	80.6	84.2	20.2	22.3
2040	77.1	81.0	17.8	19.9	79.2	82.9	19.0	21.1	81.4	84.9	20.7	22.8
2045	77.3	81.2	17.9	20.0	79.7	83.3	19.3	21.4	82.2	85.5	21.2	23.3
2050	77.6	81.4	18.0	20.1	80.1	83.7	19.6	21.7	82.9	86.2	21.7	23.8
2055	77.8	81.6	18.1	20.2	80.6	84.1	19.9	22.0	83.6	86.8	22.2	24.2
2060	78.0	81.8	18.3	20.3	81.1	84.5	20.2	22.3	84.3	87.4	22.7	24.7
2065	78.3	82.0	18.4	20.5	81.5	84.9	20.5	22.5	84.9	87.9	23.1	25.1
2070	78.5	82.2	18.5	20.6	81.9	85.3	20.7	22.8	85.5	88.4	23.5	25.5
2075	78.7	82.4	18.6	20.7	82.3	85.6	21.0	23.0	86.1	89.0	23.9	25.9
2080	78.9	82.5	18.7	20.8	82.7	86.0	21.2	23.3	86.7	89.4	24.3	26.2
2085	79.1	82.7	18.9	20.9	83.1	86.3	21.5	23.5	87.2	89.9	24.7	26.6

[a] The period life expectancy at a given age for a given year represents the average number of years of life remaining if a group of persons at that age were to experience the mortality rates for that year over the course of their remaining lives.
[b] Estimated.

14.4 Life Expectancy.   Source: Social Security Administration, Office of the Chief Actuary. SSA Bulletin, Vol 70, No. 3, 2010

Seventy-five percent of the people born since 1970 will reach at least 85 years old. As time goes on, the number of Social Security recipients and the average payout per person increase. Faced with a money system that grows debt exponentially, the retirement system cannot survive with any meaningful benefit.

	Recipients	Average per month
1979	35,012,958	$258.37
1989	39,141,080	$511.89
1999	44,595,481	$730.53
2009	52,522,819	$1,064.41

Now the Repocrats and Wankers say we only have two options to fix this.

1. Tax More
2. Reduce Benefits

Taking this 2008 tax figure of 900 billion dollars out over the next 25 years, we come up with more than 20 trillion dollars in taxes to be collected. Let's remind ourselves that this money is earned from labor, rather than invented out of thin air as the shareholders of the Federal Reserve can do. This is an enormous resource that we can use to fund various projects. Right now, this FICA tax is converted into Federal Reserve money, and depreciates by design into a fraction of its original value. With no change, this 20 trillion in effort will be stolen from the population and transferred to the shareholders of the Federal Reserve.

Here is how the theft happens:

1. People work hard and with their employer pay 15 percent of their income in FICA taxes
2. These FICA taxes are converted into computerized money that is backed by paper money.
3. Inflation will depreciate this money.
4. Eventually, this money is sent to the Wankers by paying interest on

the National Debt that was invented from thin air. The money that was lent to fund the national debt was invented from thin air, and now it is paid back with money that comes from people's labor.

5. Through funding shortfalls, the Social Security benefits are cut. by inflating the currency.

6. The Wankers use this money to buy real assets. They buy farmland, mineral rights, gold, silver, and eventually will buy all the public lands.

"I sincerely believe that banking institutions are more dangerous to our liberties than standing armies. The issuing power should be taken from the banks and restored to the people to whom it properly belongs."

Thomas Jefferson

Instead of following the Repocrats, Wankers, and bureaucrats, we can find a better solution - a third option. We can honor the promises made to the people who have been paying into the system all their lives. We can offer a decent standard of living for those who need it.

Option Three

- Put the FICA taxes into large infrastructure projects.

- Issue United States Notes (not Federal Reserve Notes), for these projects

- Make the US Notes interest free. Or, charge interest, but the interest on the US notes go to the Treasury as a tax. These interest payments on infrastructure will take the place of income taxes and eventually there will be no need for an income tax.

- The United States Notes will fund infrastructure and be retired against the project. This will keep inflation low. Power Currency is issued and used equal to the electricity output. One Gigawatt per day issues one gigawatt equivalent in Power Currency – no

175

more and no less.

- The infrastructure adds to the national wealth and will provide its own return on investment. There is no new debt from this.

- The dividends fund Social Security.

Energy backed Power Currency is a good solution for retirees. Energy costs a good proportion of income for retirees, unemployed, single mothers, etc... People below 20,000 dollars income pay ten percent of their income to cover energy, while those above 100,000 income pay one or two percent on energy.

This energy is debt free and won't exponentially increase the debt. The future funding gap is over 20 percent each year. If we use debt free money, we will eliminate the usury interest that comes from thin air issued money.

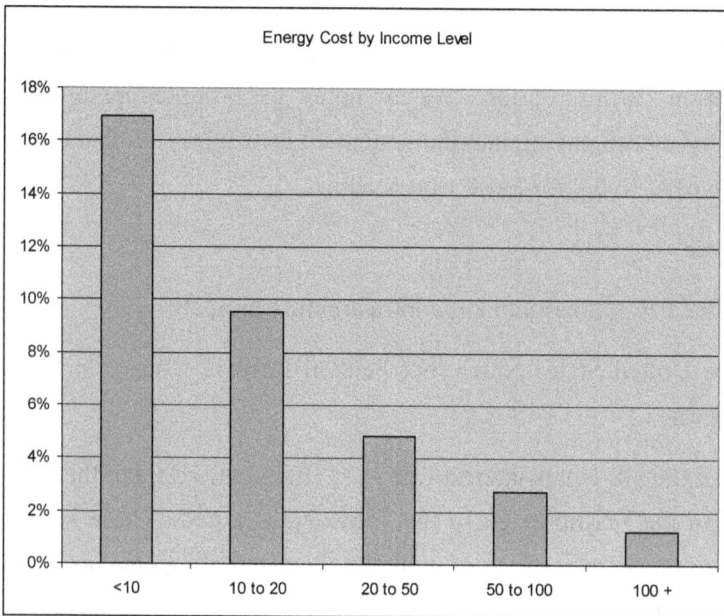

14.5 Energy Cost by income

Let's look at a typical Social Security monthly benefit:

POWER CURRENCY

Current way

Federal Reserve debt based dollars per month

New way

Part in paper money (United States money or Federal Reserve money) and part in Power Currency. For example, 80 - 90 percent in dollars and 10 - 20 percent in Power Currency.

In 2009 there are about 53 million recipients, collecting on average $1050 per month. Let's use 60 million recipients and 1200 USD per month

1000KWH per month is enough for basic needs with some left over for spending into the economy. Recipients would have enough for the following:

Air conditioner, electric heating
Kitchen appliances - refrigerators, electric stove, microwave
Washing machine, iron, dryer
50 inch TV with high end audio equipment
Computer, phone, printer, etc
Other fun stuff

The advantage with a fixed amount is as power is increased, and then less is needed to cover basic things like heating, cooling, cooking, comfort, lights, etc... Let's look at this nationally. Here is our 2010 and 2030 population projections in the USA by age groups.

Year	0-14	15-64	65+	Total
2010	62380610	207623541	40228712	310232863
2030	72959056	228452703	72091915	373503674

So take the 2030 figures which are about when out bureaucrats predict the system will die.

Let's take ten percent of that

Monthly benefit	$1,200
Paper Money	$1,000
Power Currency	$200
price per KWH	$0.20
KWH/month	1,000
Capacity needed per day	
Recipients	60,000,000
KWH/year/person	12,000
GWH per year	720,000
GWH Capacity needed	164

1,000,000 KWH = 1 GWH

This new capacity needed is equal to about fifteen percent of what we have now. It is also equal to the new electricity power capacity that China is constructing in the next 24 months.

Other scenarios can be derived from this.

To allocate 5 KWH per day to everyone in the country.

5 KWH per day per day for children.

10 KWH per day to 65 yrs and older

10 KWH per day to unemployed

At this point, it starts looking a bit Socialist. Keep in mind that the money for this comes from the FICA taxes that are being paid anyway. This is a far better solution for the taxpayer and the country, than putting FICA taxes into computer entry paper that will be transferred to the shareholders of the Federal Reserve.

Here is another scenario. We reduce the amount per day, but include children. We get the following scenario. All sorts of scenarios can be developed.

	0-14	65+	Total
Population in 2030	72,959,056	72,091,915	373,503,674
KWH/person	10	10	
KWH/ day	729,590,560	720,919,150	
365 days	Per year		
2030	266,301,000,000	263,135,000,000	529,436,000,000

Another consideration is to push for a dramatic increase in energy production. If done, then the amount needed to support basic energy needs becomes quite small. If we increase our capacity five-fold, then the amount needed would be less than three percent of future capacity.

2010 Level	4,000 TW	13.2%
Future Level	20,000 TW	2.6%

So the Social Security gap can be covered with as low as 2.6 percent of our electricity. This is including children in the system of social services. If we take them out, then the amount is about one percent

Those FICA taxes are socialist in any case, so we might as well use them for productive purposes.

Less than 25 percent of our FICA taxes is needed for large national projects like Train Grid and doubling our energy capacity. 200 Billion of FICA taxes would be enough to build over 100 GWH in production and 1000 miles of high speed rail per year. Each year we add another 100 GWH and 1000 miles. In twenty years, we have 20,000 miles of high speed rail built with FICA taxes and financed as we showed in the Energy Homestead chapter.

It would be hard to imagine high unemployment in a situation like that.

Eventually, we would more than enough to solve basic needs, and move onto a system of abundance, not one of scarcity.

The rest of the FICA taxes can be used for ventures to Mars, cancer cures, and so forth.

The alternative is to put our FICA into paper money that will depreciate into nothing.

POWER CURRENCY ECONOMY

Huge increases in energy will lead to great prosperity. So what would the impact on GDP be for a doubling of energy output? Let's look all the things we can do with this extra capacity. We open up all kinds of new fields in space and bring hard to believe prosperity. Some examples:

- Agriculture – aquaculture, greenhouses
- Social programs - Subsidies to schools and hospitals; Help the aged, poor
- Medicine. New machines and treatments. Very high tech solutions for curing disease and extending quality of life.
- Transportation. High speed rail. All kinds of innovations in transport. Space travel.
- Pollution. Dramatic reduction in fossil fuels
- Entertainment - Wall sized plasma screen TV's

Many people have made predictions about the future of energy. Google, EPRI and EIA for example see a growth rate of one or two percent per year. This would bring up to about 1,300 GWH of capacity by 2030, or where China will be in 2014. We can see a much higher growth rate driven by distributed energy, entrepreneurs, financial incentives, etc... This will lead to a much higher growth in our energy production capability.

EPRI did a study where they predict these changes over 20 or 30 years. The technology exists now and will be brought to market as the entrepreneurs and customers push for it. The market will dictate this, not some agency in Washington DC.

	Installed Base	Growth Rate	Renewable Share
Google	1,200	1%	40%
EIA	1,250	1.1%	25%
EPRI	1,250	1.1%	25%
P2P Electric	4,000	6%	60%
Power Currency	20,000	10%	90%

15.1 Projections for 2030

In fact with some technology breakthroughs we could see an installed capacity go to 100 or 1000 times the 2010 level.

In the next twenty years the following are possible

- gas powered cars are gone – become electric and hybrid
- gas and diesel powered trucks are gone – become electric or hybrid
- energy up ten times
- pollution cut in half
- new forms of commerce take hold

Looking at recent history, production and consumption of energy in the USA

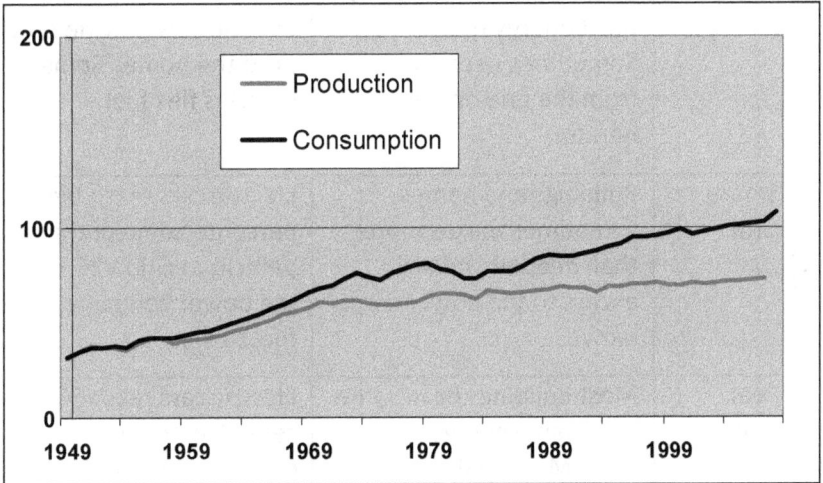

15.2 Production and Consumption Quadrillion BTUs

With some small sustained shifts, PHEV and all electric vehicles will do-minate the market by 2030. People will move to electric for the following reasons

1. It is cheaper to operate and maintain
2. Performance is better
3. Vehicle to Grid will open up new business models and further reduce costs for homeowners
4. reduced costs for fleets and large trucks
5. Less pollution

	Stationary	Moving
Phase	Homes, farms, buildings, roads..	Cars, trucks, trains, ships ..
20th Century	Traditional Power Grid	Cars and trucks run on gasoline and diesel
Hybrid	Some locations can power most energy needs. Sometimes need to buy from the grid or use a generator	Some hybrid and small electric cars provide power to the home. Some vehicles flex fuel.
Smart Grid	Buildings and homes sometimes makes more than needed and sell excess to the power company	Electric cars reach five percent. Some of them do Vehicle to Grid V2G with the power company. Flex fuel to all.
Peer to Peer Electricity	Most buildings have some renewable energy production. Many make more than they need and do P2P Electric exchanges - buildings, grids, vehicles	Electric cars reach 50 percent. Electric trucks start coming. TrainGrid. Vehicle to Vehicle V2V energy.
Power Currency	Home to home exchange of energy and energy backed money is easy and common	Electric cars are over fifty percent and easily exchange electricity credits back and forth

15.3 Five Phases to Get to Power Currency

Here is how we can see the future if we focus on increasing our renewable energy mix between five and ten percent each year, compounded.

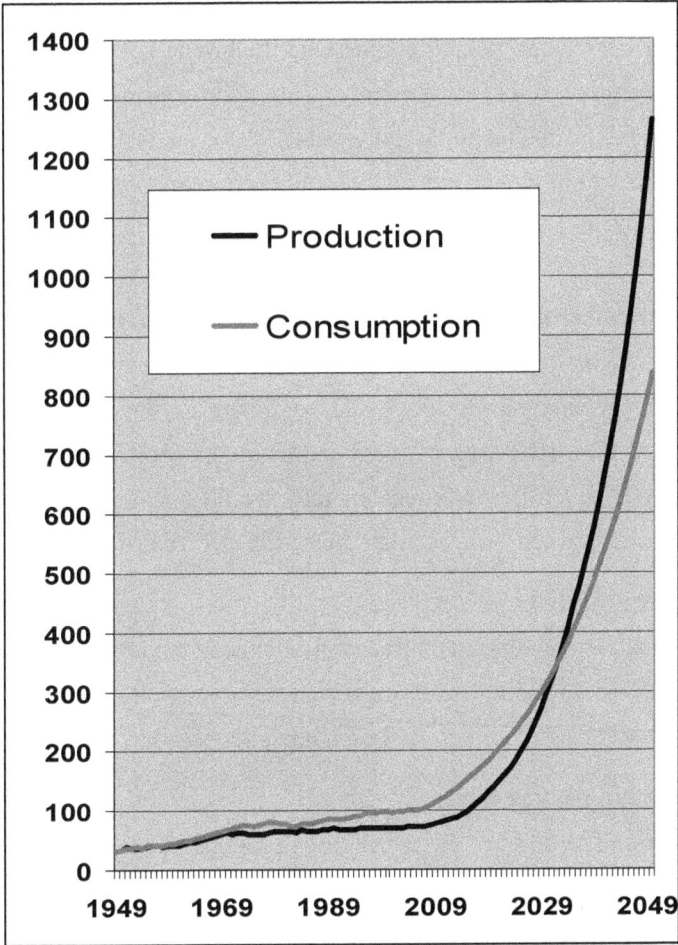

15.4 Future Production and Consumption Quadrillion BTUs

This is achievable with no increase in the use of fossil fuels. The Cap and Trade people will have a dilemma. There is an abundance of energy but it is clean. Five or ten percent compounded is not hard to achieve.

If you asked Alexander Graham Bell to look at the current communications technology, he would be amazed. From a simple telegraph system to now, we have seen the Morse code transformed to streaming video worldwide.

If you were to ask Henry Ford and Thomas Edison to look at the current state of the electric grid, the car engine, and the money system, they would question why things look so familiar. The electric grid is a centralized monster using the same technologies as the 1920's, the internal combustion engine still fires fuel to move a piston, and the money system is still debt based and centrally controlled.

Many industries behemoths are now history. Big telecom has had to adapt. The music industry sees record shops go bankrupt and new business models take over. China stores have had to adapt to the demand of the customers and they offer free wireless connections now at McDonalds and Starbucks. AOL ruled the internet, but they would not open their mind to the possibilities, and they stayed with their cash cow dial-up service.

The new energy systems will replace the old giants. Low cost battery, low cost solar, and new inventions. Renewable energy technologies will continue to improve. In the future electric cars, hybrids, solar cells, wind, bio mass and other forms of energy will be made and stored at lower costs.

Here are some of the key drivers.

> Chips: The number of micro chips produced each year is growing exponentially

> Communication: Now there are over one billion people on the internet, and if we add in smart phones, half the planet is connected. The other trend is the internet of things - pipelines, shipping containers, trucks, and cars

> Smart: With all these chips and the communications, it is natural that we will have some sophisticated software to manage the whole system. The systems are getting intelligent.

Technology advances lead to cheaper and better. An example is the cost for solar energy. The cost of production is dropping steadily. These trends point to a future that has an abundance of energy.

Cost per watt

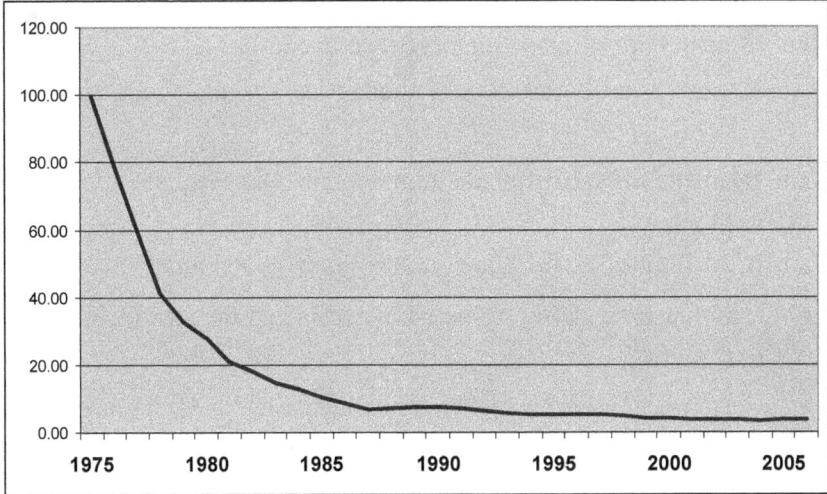

15.5 Tech, Cost curve

Things we can do in 2010, which would be difficult or expensive in 2000:

- Scale of the system in the tens of millions of nodes.
- Millions of computers talk to each other automatically.
- Energy producing machines (wind, solar, generators, etc) can talk straight to computers on a large scale.
- The whole process should operate seamlessly so users do not care how the transactions happen and should be as simple to operate as possible.
- System is fault tolerant so if one part of the network goes down, then the others can take over and make sure things happen as they should.
- Security is strong and not allows hackers or fraud to disrupt and defraud any of the participants.
- Authentication in place at every point on the network. Most of this

is built into the various nodes such as energy devices batteries and smart meters.

- Passwords, digital certificates, smart cards, and biometrics tie into the system.
- Identity must be confirmed between the parties and all devices using any or a combination of biometrics, tokens, smart cards and online tools.
- Detailed accounting for the transactions is handled locally or centrally.
- Billions of micropayments are collected and dispersed.
- Data Integrity. Every resource has metadata for identification and transactions.
- Priority data. Who is higher in the hierarchy, and who must listen to whom. Then also some conditions in place

Innovation.

We will see thousands of new products related to energy.

- Charging kits for cars.
- Retrofitting homes and buildings to charge electric cars
- New kits that will load up electricity slowly, and fast charge cars
- Beneficiaries
- Electricians
- Homebuilders
- Contractors
- Homeowners

Go to www.uspto.gov or www.google.com/patents and look at the patent database. These patents (the more recent the better) become blueprints for 'new' technology. There are enough inventions that are off patent that you could make very good products. The Google site is a good place to start.

It is much easier to search and download pdf versions of the patents.

1. Look back to inventions prior to twenty years ago. So if today is January 1, 2011, you will look at patents prior to January 1, 1991.
2. Put in you select keywords and pick out a few.
3. Study those; come up with your own ideas to make the invention better.
4. Then after you have your own ideas, search again within the patents within the past twenty years. If you find your idea is unique, then you are onto something. If you find someone has already thought of it, then you need to decide to either contact them to license it, or sell it, or try to make your idea even better.

This is a great learning exercise and you might hit a grand slam! Sometimes the 20 year old patented ideas will be good enough and cheap enough to build. If you have a device costing 100 dollars and provide 1 KWH of value, it is better than one costing 2500 dollars and provides 2 KWH of value.

The EV1 car they built twenty years ago is now off patent and all that technology is free to the public. General Motors have no choice now. They must build electric cars.

There are thousands of ways to pay for this.
- Individuals can invest. They put in 1 to a 10,000 dollars in Federal Reserve Notes and receive a certain amount of KWH back each month. This can be financed and offer a positive cash flow.
- Taxes. Social Security taxes are put toward such largest projects. SSA recipients receive Frollars and KWH each month as their pension
- National credit. Issue money tax free through 50 year bonds and pay it off through electricity credits as they are spent

- Military budgets to support the energy needs of the bases in the area.
- Casinos set up schemes to let people buy energy, and then they can gamble these credits at the casinos.

Our nation has had three types of money systems.

1. Private sector production based - from colonial times up to about 1900. This system is reflected in the Coinage Act of 1792. The Government established the weights and measures of the money. The government set up mints that anyone could use to take raw gold and silver and coin into standard money. This is free market and very anti-collectivist.
2. National system - Civil War to 1971. We see more control at the Federal Level. This system had some advantages to collect resources and build large projects like the transcontinental railroad, and interstate highway system.
3. Debt based usury system - 1913 until today. This started in 1913, and gained grounds with the death of the gold standard in 1971, and is quickly accelerating after 2008.

The first is free market. The last two are collectivist in nature, with varying degrees of severity. Our current form of collectivism sees the transfer of wealth from the middle class to a small group of wealthy people. This is done through taxes and printing of money.

The duty of the Government is to establish an honest money system. This will clean out the debts and let us reach the future prosperity we are meant to find. Here in Table 15.6 is our statistics from Chapter One, Table 1.2. We take the old numbers and build a scenario how Power Currency could develop in the future. Power Currency takes the position as hard money, money that is a commodity.

	Hard Money Commodity Gold Silver, Metal Coins		United States Money Government U.S. Dollars		Bank Money Private Federal Reserve Dollars (Frollars)	
1800	16	62%	0	0%	10	38%
1850	147	53%	0	0%	131	47%
1870	90	12%	357	46%	328	42%
1890	485	34%	764	53%	182	13%
1910	846	27%	1617	51%	687	22%
1930	794	18%	1670	37%	2054	45%
1950	1495	6%	2539	9%	22848	85%
1970	6128	11%	522	1%	47656	88%
1990	2000	1%	0	0%	254400	99%
2010	3000	0%	0	0%	873300	100%
	Hard Money Power Currency		United States Money U.S. Dollars, State Money		Bank Money Frollars	
2020		**10%**		**20%**		**70%**
2030		**20%**		**30%**		**50%**
2040		**30%**		**40%**		**30%**
Tax Source	Kilowatts from transactions		FICA Taxes, Pro-duction, TrainGrid, Energy Homes-teads		Frollar Income Taxes, Tobin Tax-es, Wanker Prison earnings.	
National Debt	No Debt		No US Dollars to pay any Frollar debt		Any shortfall in paying off Frollar debt, print more Frollars	

15.6 Future Hard Money, US Dollars and Federal Reserve Dollars.

Taxes come from the type of money itself. US dollars cannot pay off debt made from thin air generated Federal Reserve dollars.

1. Debt based currency. Federal Reserve Notes remain in place and used to pay off the national debt. Any payments for interest on the debt come directly from more Federal Reserve Notes. There is a restrictions that no labor, land, homes or assets ever be forfeited to Federal Reserve Notes. Taxes from financial speculation and wanker prison labor is used to pay off the national debt.

2. Government issued money. This is for infrastructure projects primarily. All Social Security taxes go to debt free systems to build infrastructure.

3. Power Currency. Energy backed currency produced by anyone. This is the basic free market economy.

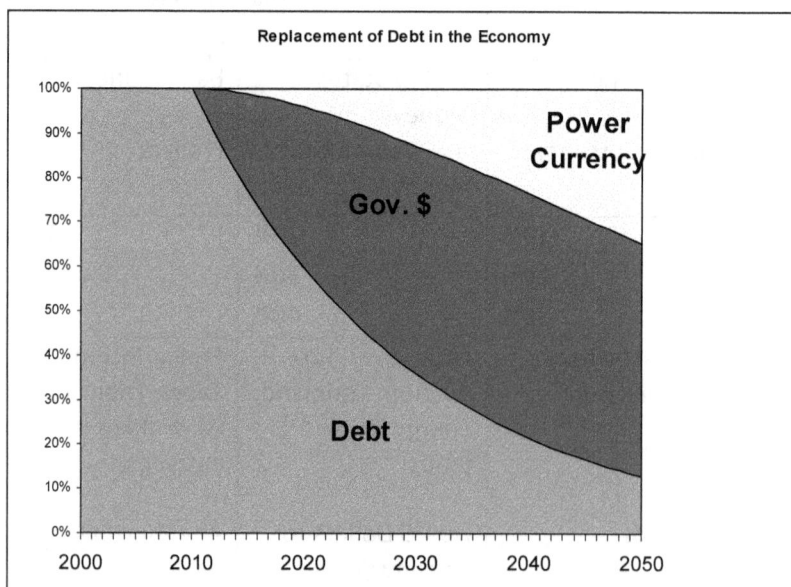

15.7 Future money out to 2050

There will be winners and losers in this change. If you own or rent a home, you will be a winner. If you own a car, you will be a winner. States and Cities will win. Electric Utilities will be big winners. All banks except for the top five banks will win. Wankers will lose. They will need to get a job, or learn how to live in prison. Repocrats will lose, as they will not be able to print money at will and direct to their cronies. The Department of War will lose, but the Department of Defense will win.

The situation now shows that we have all the tools necessary to make this happen. Everyone uses electricity, and nearly everyone has a home and car. Here is how this can work out over the next twenty years.

2010

	Electricity	Fuels	Engines
Collectivists	99%	95%	10%
People	1%	5%	90%

15.8 Collectivists vs People 2010

- Electricity is dominated by large centralized power plants that deliver electricity through a grid. It is very centralized and controlled and old.

- Fuels are primarily oil, but also include coal, natural gas, and renewable fuels like wind, hydro resources, and solar.

- Engines are cars, trucks, trains, ships, wind turbines and power plants for energy.

2030

	Electricity	Fuels	Engines
Collectivists	20%	30%	10%
People	80%	70%	90%

15.9 Collectivists vs People 2030

- Electricity now is produced by anyone, and distributed peer to peer.

- Fuels are produced in America and there is a big shift to bio-fuels and renewable systems.

- Engines stay the same.

By 2030, our national debt will be 90 percent retired. The remaining debt will be there to keep some form of liquidity for trade.

Power Currency is the money for the 21st Century. It uses the same economic system set up by our founding fathers

It can:

>Wipe out the national debt
>Fund infrastructure projects such as high speed rail and new power grids
>Increase our energy supply 10 to 100 times
>Cut pollution
>Get off foreign oil imports
>Turn your car into a money making machine
>Fund Social Security forever
>Open new investment alternatives
>Slay the debt dragon

Power Currency is freedom.

POWER CURRENCY

ENDNOTES

---

[i] http://www.chinadaily.com.cn/usa/business/energy.html

[ii] www.eia.doe.gov

[iii] Timberlake, Richard, "The Central Banking Role of Clearinghouse Associations", Journal of Money, Credit and Banking, Feb 1984, 1 – 15

Horwitz, Steven, Competitive Currencies, Legal Restrictions, and the Origins of the Fed: Some Evidence from the Panic of 1907", "Competitive Currencies and the Origins of the Fed", 2001, Page 639 - 649

[iv] Much of the historical statistics used throughout this book can be found starting here http://www.census.gov/compendia/statab/past_years.html Start with the bicentennial edition and some other years. There is a lot of overlap, so you can usually verify quite fast.

[v] http://www.constitution.org/uslaw/coinage1792.txt

[vi] Pulled from multiple sources...   Andrew Carnegie, US Government, Textbooks

[vii] http://www.ca8.uscourts.gov/opndir/05/04/042357P.pdf

[viii] http://www.webofdebt.com/excerpts/introduction.php

[ix] http://www.historycentral.com/Documents/Clinton/SigningNaFTA.html

[x] www.tencent.com

[xi] http://english.people.com.cn/200701/12/eng20070112_340681.html

http://www.pbc.gov.cn/english/detail.asp?col=6400&ID=611

[xii] Title: The Writings of Abraham Lincoln, v7
Author: Abraham Lincoln

Release Date: June, 2001 [Etext #2659]

http://www.gutenberg.org/files/2659/old/7linc11.txt

[xiii] Money Supply data from People's Bank of China website www.pbc.gov.cn
metals data from http://minerals.usgs.gov/minerals/pubs/country/asia.html#cb

[xiv] We expect the wind to be blowing 34 percent of the time, which is a low estimate. So with 34 percent, multiplied by 24 hours and 365 days, we get 3000 MW hours worth for each MWH installed.

ONLINE RESOURCES: GOVERNMENT

U.S. Census

    www.census.gov

    http://www.census.gov/compendia/statab/past_years.html

US Geological Survey

    www.usgs.gov

Department of Energy Information

    www.eia.doe.gov

Bureau of Labor Statistics

    www.bls.gov

Department of Transportation

    www.bts.gov

FDIC

    www.fdic.gov

Comptroller

    www.occ.treas.gov

Treasury Department

    www.treasury.gov

Department of Energy — Federal Energy Management Program (FEMP)

    www.eren.doe.gov/femp

Department of Energy — Distributed Energy Resources Program

    www.eren.doe.gov/der

Department of Energy — Office of Power Technologies

    www.eren.doe.gov/power

FEMP New Technology Demonstration Program (NTDP)

    www.eren.doe.gov/femp/prodtech/newtechdemo.html

FEMP Renewable Energy Resources

    www.eren.doe.gov/femp/techassist/renewenergy.html

Federal Incentives for Commercial Solar Applications

    www.mdv-seia.org/federal_incentives.htm

Green Power Network — State Net Metering Programs

www.eren.doe.gov/greenpower/netmetering/index.shtml

Making Connections: Case Studies of Interconnection Barriers and their Impact on Distributed Power Projects

www.nrel.gov/docs/fy00osti/28053.pdf

ONLINE RESOURCES: INDUSTRY

Federal Reserve Bank

www.federalreserve.gov

JP Morgan

www.jpmorgan.com

Citibank

www.citibank.com

Bank of America

www.bankofamerica.com

Wells Fargo

www.wellsfargo.com

Goldman Sachs

www.gs.com

Federal Reserve Bank of New York

www.newyorkfed.org

Federal Reserve Bank of Boston

www.bos.frb.org

Federal Reserve Bank of Philadelphia

www.philadelphiafed.org

Federal Reserve Bank of Cleveland

www.clevelandfed.org

Federal Reserve Bank of Richmond

www.richmondfed.org

Federal Reserve Bank of Atlanta

www.frbatlanta.org

Federal Reserve Bank of Chicago

www.chicagofed.org

Federal Reserve Bank of St. Louis

www.stlouisfed.org

Federal Reserve Bank of Minneapolis

www.minneapolisfed.org

Federal Reserve Bank of Kansas City

www.kansascityfed.org

Federal Reserve Bank of Dallas

www.dallasfed.org

Federal Reserve Bank of San Francisco

www.frbsf.org

Edison Electric Institute

www.eei.org

Energy-efficient Product Information

www.energystar.gov

Engine and Turbine Manufacturers Directory

www.dieselpub.com/catalog/

United States Fuel Cell Council

www.usfcc.com

Solar Energy Industries Association

www.seia.org

Database of State Incentives for Renewable Energy

www.dsireusa.org

American Wind Energy Association

www.awea.org

Electricity Storage Association

www.energystorage.org/

Distributed Power Coalition of America

www.distributedpower.com

National Association of Regulatory Utility Commissioners

www.naruc.org

Institute of Electrical and Electronics Engineers

www.ieee.org

Carnegie Mellon Software Engineering Institute, Smart Grid Maturity Model: Results Survey, v1.0, June 2009

http://www.sei.cmu.edu/smartgrid

BIBLIOGRAPHY

A Primer on Money, A U.S. Government publication, August 5, 1964; produced for the Committee on Banking and Currency, House of Representatives, pg 1-5.

Allen, Larry. The Encyclopedia of Money, 2nd Edition. ABC-CLIO, LLC, 2009

Anstey, Frank. Money Power. Fraser and Jenkinson Printers and Publishers, 1921

Boardman, John, and Sauser, Brian. Systems Thinking - Coping with 21st Century Problems. CRC Press, 2008

Borbely, Ann-Marie and Kreider, Jan F. Distributed Generation, The Power Paradigm for the New Millennium. CRC Press, 2001

Box, Harry. Set Lighting Technician's Handbook, Film Lighting Equipment, Practice, and Electrical Distribution, Fourth Edition. Elsevier, Inc. 2010

BP Statistical Review of World Energy, June 2010 http://www.bp.com/statisticalreview

Brandt, Loren, and Thomas J. Sargent. Interpreting New Evidence about China and U.S. Silver Purchases. Journal of Monetary Economics 23 (1989): 31–51.

Brons, Wilbur J. Bankers Monthly, Three Centuries of Money, Men and Banks. September 1952.

Brown, Ellen Hodgson. Web of Debt, Fourth Edition. Third Millenium Press, 2010

Buford, John F. and Yu, Heather, and Lue, Eng Keong. P2P Networking and Applications. Elsevier Inc. 2009

Cambridge Energy Research Associates, "Construction Costs for New Power Plants Continue to Escalate: IHS CERA Power Capital Costs Index" (press release,

May 27, 2008)

Carnegie, Andrew. The ABC of Money. The North American Review, circa 1900

Caromel, Denis. A Theory of Distributed Objects. Springer-Verlag Berlin Heidelberg, 2005

Chirn, Dan. The Homeowner's Guide to Renewable Energy. New Society Publishers , 2006

Coogan, Gertrude M. Money Creators, Who Creates Money? Who Should Create It? LCCN 67-28926, 1935

Da Rosa. Fundamentals of Renewable Energy Processes, ISBN 9780120885107, 2005

David Pong, Editor. Encyclopedia of Modern China. Charles Scribner's Sons, 2009

Dreamtech Software Team. Instant Messaging Systems, Cracking the Code. Wiley Publishing, Inc. 2002

Electricity 101, Edison Electric Institute (EEI) www.eei.org.

ETIENNE DE LA BOETIE, The Politics of Obedience: The Discourse on Voluntary Servitude. Black Rose Books, Montreal, 2008.

Federal Reserve Bank of Chicago. MODERN MONEY MECHANICS, A Workbook on Bank Reserves and Deposit Expansion. This complete booklet was originally produced and distributed free by: Public Information Center Federal Reserve Bank of Chicago
for Electric-Drive Vehicles, 1009299 (Palo Alto, CA,

Greco, Thomas. The End of Money and the Future of Civilization. Chelsea Green Publishing, 2009

Griffin, G. Edward. The Creature From Jekyll Island: A Second Look at the Federal Reserve. American Media 2002.

Hobart, Mary. A Scientific Exposure of the Errors in Our Monetary System. The People's Call Publishing Co. 1891

Holloway, Edward Holloway. How Guernsey Beat the Bankers. Economic Reform Club, London, 1958

Hosein, Imran. The Gold Dinar and Silver Dirham: Islam and the Future of Money. www.ummahzone.com

Hostetler, Merle. 75 Years of American Finance, A Graphical Representation 1861 to 1935. St Louis Federal Reserve Bank

Howard, Tharon. Praise of Design to Thrive: Creating Social Networks and On-line Communities that Last. Morgan Kaufmann, Publishers. 2010

Lietaer, Bernard. Complementary Currencies in Japan Today: History, Originality and Relevance. International Journal of Community Currency Research. Vol.8, pp.1-23

Lietaer, Bernard. The Future of Money, Random House, London, 2000

Liu, Ray, and Sadek, Ahmed, and Su, Weifeng. Cooperative Communications and Networking. Cambridge University Press, 2009

M.A. Kromer and J.B. Heywood, Electric Powertrains: Opportunities and Challenges in the U.S. Light-Duty Vehicle Fleet, Massachusetts Institute of Technology, 2007

Moore, Dana and Wright, William. Jabber Developer's Handbook. Sams Publishing, 2004.

Morgan Stanley, "Leading Wall Street Banks Establish The Carbon Principles" (Press Release, February 4, 2008), web site www.morganstanley.com/about/press/articles/6017.html.

Mullins, Eustace. Secrets of the Federal Reserve. 1952

Nersesian, Roy, and Sharpe, M. E. Energy for the 21st Century, A Comprehensive Guide to Conventional and Alternative Sources. Armonk, New York 2007

North, Peter. Money and Liberation, The Micropolitics of Alternative Currency Movements. University of Minnesota Press, 2007

Pansini, Anthony. Guide to Electrical Power Distribution Systems, 6th Edition. THE FAIRMONT PRESS, INC. 2006

Paul, Ron. End The Fed. Grand Central Publishing, 2009.

Quigley, Carroll. Tragedy and Hope. GSG Books and Associates

Rizzoni. Principles and Applications of Electrical Engineering. McGraw-Hill, 2006

Rothbard, Murray N. The Case Against the Fed, Ludwig von Mises Institute, 1994

Schauf, Thomas D. The Federal Reserve is PRIVATELY OWNED, 1992

Standard Catalog of World Paper Money, General Issues – 1368 to 1960. Krause Publications, 2008

Standard Catalog of World Paper Money, Modern Issues. Krause Publications, 2008

Taylor, Ian J. and Harrison, Andrew B. From P2P and Grids to Services on the Web, Evolving Distributed Communities, Second Edition. Springer-Verlag London Limited 2009

The Biodiesel Handbook. AOCS Press, 2005

U.S. Department of Energy, Alternative Fuels Data Center, "Alternative Fueling Station Total Counts by State and Fuel Type," web site www.afdc.energy.

Using Distributed Energy Resources A How-To Guide for Federal Facility Managers, 2008

Walbert, M. W. The Coming Battle, 1899

Xuemin Shen, Heather Yu, John Buford. Handbook of Peer-to-Peer Networking. ⌐ c Springer Science+Business Media, LLC 2010

Yang. Bioprocessing for Value-Added Products from Renewable Resources, ISBN 9780444521149, 2007

Zepp-LaRouche, Helga. The Historical Roots Of Green Fascism, EIR Investigation, April 13, 2007

ABOUT THE AUTHOR

James P Rogers works in China and the United States. He has experience in a variety of industries including automotive, IT and energy. James graduated from West Point with a degree in Engineering. He served in the US Army in Infantry, Intelligence and Psychological Operations.